Praise for
Do you matter?

"Telling great stories through design leads to experiences your customers will love. This book uncovers the path to world class design that matters to people and to profits that shareholders treasure."
   –Sam Lucente *vice president, HP Design*

"Being design-driven is not about just making beautiful products. It is about how a company can deliver a positive emotional idea to the customer. This book will tell you how to embed great design in your business culture."
   –Sang-yeon Lee *director, Samsung Design America*

"If your interest is brand and design, *Do You Matter?* dares to ask the tough questions, and ventures to answer them with insight and clarity. Well done Brunner and Emery!"
   –Todd Wood *vice president, industrial design, Research In Motion*

"With their brutally honest assessment of many of the brands and products that litter our lives, Brunner and Emery leave no doubt that customer-centered experience design is the key to transforming business. You must read this book."
   –Darrel Rhea *CEO, Cheskin Added Value*

"No one knows industrial design and its impact on companies better than Robert Brunner. In this book, Brunner and Emery show why design matters. This is a must read for anyone needing to understand the powerful impact of design."
   –Phil Baker *author,* From Concept to Consumer

Do you matter?

Do you matter?
How great design will make people love your company

Robert Brunner
and
Stewart Emery

With Russ Hall

Vice President, Publisher: Tim Moore
Associate Publisher and Director of Marketing: Amy Neidlinger
Editorial Assistant: Myesha Graham
Development Editor: Russ Hall
Operations Manager: Gina Kanouse
Digital Marketing Manager: Julie Phifer
Publicity Manager: Laura Czaja
Assistant Marketing Manager: Megan Colvin
Marketing Assistant: Brandon Smith
Cover and Interior Designer: Pentagram
Managing Editor: Kristy Hart
Project Editor: Chelsey Marti
Copy Editor: Krista Hansing
Proofreader: Water Crest Publishing
Indexer: Erika Millen
Manufacturing Buyer: Dan Uhrig

FT Press offers excellent discounts on this book when ordered in quantity for bulk
purchases or special sales. For more information, please contact U.S. Corporate and
Government Sales, 1-800-382-3419, corpsales@pearsontechgroup.com. For sales outside
the U.S., please contact International Sales at international@pearson.com.

Printed in the United States of America

First Printing August 2008

ISBN-10: 0-13-714244-7
ISBN-13: 978-0-13-714244-6

Pearson Education LTD.
Pearson Education Australia PTY, Limited.
Pearson Education Singapore, Pte. Ltd.
Pearson Education North Asia, Ltd.
Pearson Education Canada, Ltd.
Pearson Educatión de Mexico, S.A. de C.V.
Pearson Education—Japan
Pearson Education Malaysia, Pte. Ltd.

Library of Congress Cataloging-in-Publication Data

Brunner, Robert, 1958-

  Do you matter? : how great design will make people love your company / Robert Brunner,
Stewart Emery.

    p. cm.

  ISBN 0-13-714244-7 (hbk. : alk. paper) 1. Design, Industrial. 2. New products. 3.
Industrial design coordination. 4. Branding (Marketing) I. Emery, Stewart, 1941- II. Title.

  TS171.B79 2009

  745.2--dc22

                              2008015040

7

Your Products and Services Are Talking to People

How to make sure that they're saying the right thing • What is a design language? • Why is it important? • How you actually create and manage your companies design language • Thinking strategically • Effective design strategy • How to think about design as a business weapon • Building your product brand.

8

Building a Design-Driven Culture

Why good design is everybody's job • The importance of culture to design • Why changing culture takes time • Why we need risk support instead of risk management • Why risk should be understood—not avoided • How innovative design can define new ground that is valued by your customers • How your company can use design to carve out new space • How to manage design from the top • Why great design requires faith and commitment • How leadership is essential to great design • How to manage creative resources to get the best from them.

9

Go Forth and Matter

About the Authors

Robert Brunner's career as an industrial designer is iconic in the high technology arena. As director of industrial design at Apple Computer, he founded the Industrial Design Group and developed the original Macintosh PowerBook, Newton, and 20th Anniversary Mac—prelude to the iMac. As a partner at Pentagram, one of the world's most influential design firms, he worked with Fortune 500 companies, including Nike, Microsoft, Hewlett Packard, Dell, and Nokia, as well as developed new products for many global enterprises. In early 2007, Robert founded Ammunition, a product design, brand, and interactive development consultancy. His product designs have won numerous awards from the Industrial Designers Society of America and *Business Week*, including eight best of category awards. His work is included in the permanent design collection of the Museum of Modern Art (MoMA). Robert also teaches advanced product design at Stanford University.

Stewart Emery is coauthor of the international bestseller, *Success Built to Last*. He has a lifetime of experience as an entrepreneur, creative director, corporate culture consultant, and executive coach. He has conducted coaching interviews with more than 12,000 people in the last three decades and is considered one of the fathers of the Human Potential Movement. Stewart serves as Visiting Professor at the John F. Kennedy University School of Management. Author of two other best-selling books, *Actualizations: You Don't Have to Rehearse to Be Yourself* and *The Owners Manual For Your Life*, Stewart Emery has led workshops, seminars, and delivered keynotes all over the world. As a consultant, he asked questions that lead MasterCard to its legendary "priceless" campaign.

Dedication

I'd like to dedicate this book to two very important people in my life. First, to my father Russell, a dedicated engineer who instilled in me a fascination of how things work and whose excellence in his career has always inspired me.

Second (and not least) to my wonderful wife Elizabeth, who supports me every day of my life, and who constantly reminds me that I can do anything I want if I set myself to the task.

Robert Brunner
May 2008

To Joan, who is my best friend, partner, and wife. She continues to remind me that it is the quality of our experience of being alive that truly matters. I am deeply grateful for our life together.

And to the memory of my parents and godparents. They inspired me to love literature, music, and design. They introduced me to the adventures of the creative process.

Stewart Emery
May 2008

Acknowledgments

As we reviewed our conversations and work with talented people who are committed to using great design to resource wonderful experiences for people all over the world, we were constantly reminded that a single good idea takes sometimes hundreds or even thousands of gifted people to achieve exceptional implementation. In the spirit of this reality we're grateful for all the talented people who have worked with us to make this book possible. Many have become good friends.

Tim Moore, who is vice president & publisher of Wharton School Publishing and FT Press imprints, provided access to the resources of Pearson, the world's largest publisher. With great generosity of spirit and endless patience, Tim supported us every step of the way.

Equally important, he made a great team available to *Do You Matter?* We give special thanks to Christina Brianik (permissions specialist), Megan Colvin (assistant marketing manager), Krista Hansing (copy editor), Kristy Hart (managing editor), Gina Kanouse (operations manager), Sarah Kearns (proofreader), Chelsey Marti (project editor),

Erika Millen (indexer), Amy Neidlinger (associate publisher and director of marketing), Julie Phifer (digital marketing manager), Brandon Smith (marketing assistant), and Dan Uhrig (manufacturing buyer).

Russ Hall (our writing partner) brought the magical touch of a storyteller to the pages of a business book with the result that we really enjoy reading this book ourselves!

Big thanks to Michael Bierut and Yve Ludwig at Pentagram New York who designed the cover and format for the book. As well as Amy Neiman who worked the design with us here in San Francisco.

We are also grateful to Kit Hinrichs at Pentagram San Francisco who helped us greatly in researching case studies for the book, along with his writing partner Delphine Hirasuna.

Thanks also to Bill Burnett at Stanford University for indirectly providing the spark when he asked Robert to teach there, and thus created the opportunity to ask students the questions that led to the book idea.

Appreciation goes to Coralie Langston-Jones of Social Blueprint and Laura Czaja of Pearson for helping us get the word out on this book.

And a special call out to the team at Ammunition who not only provided support to our many sessions in the "fishbowl" conference room, but also put up with Robert being totally distracted from his regular job for weeks at a time. And thanks to Meghan Durney and Margaret Kessler for coordinating so many things for us.

We especially want to thank Phil Baker for introducing us to each other and suggesting we collaborate on a book to present great design as a total concept. Phil has been a good friend to each of us across the span of years and is a tireless champion of excellent design as a strategy to have customers love a company. A gifted engineer with a good eye, Phil has taken many an idea from concept to consumer.

With gratitude,

Robert Brunner and **Stewart Emery**
San Francisco, California
June 2008

Design Matters

Design is the "in" mantra—so what does this mean exactly, and why do you care?

In 1997, shortly after Steve Jobs returned to Apple, Dell's founder and chairman, Michael S. Dell, was asked at the Gartner Symposium and ITxpo97 how he would fix financially troubled Apple. "What would I do?" Dell said. "I'd shut it down and give the money back to the shareholders."

He had no idea he'd be eating those words just ten years later when Apple's market capitalization surpassed not just Dell's $64 billion ($47 billion as we write this), but IBM's as well. In mid-2007, Apple was the most valuable computer maker in the world. Its market capitalization stood at nearly $162 billion, $6 billion more than that of industry heavyweight IBM. At that same time, Apple's market cap was the fourth largest among technology companies, lagging behind only Cisco ($189 billion), Google ($208 billion), and Microsoft ($290 billion).

The message: "Apple matters."

The question: "What's to learn?"

On the second day after Jobs came back to Apple, Tim Bajarin, recognized as a leading analyst and futurist covering the field of personal computers and consumer technology, was invited to meet with him. One of the questions Bajarin asked Jobs was how he planned to get the computer maker back on the road to profitability. To his surprise, one of the foundational solutions offered was "industrial design." At the time, this made no sense. However, Apple soon introduced the head-turning iMacs with their bold colors, which threw the stodgy industry and its boring beige PCs for a loop. Apple followed up with the introduction of the iPod, ever-sleeker iMacs, and the iPhone, hailed by *PC Magazine* columnist Lance Ulanoff as "the most important product of the still-young 21st century." Now the company is shaking up the notebook market with the thin, light, and stylish MacBook Air, and has taken on the video rental market with the Apple TV.

Apple has built a design-driven culture that knows how to connect with its customers in a deeply emotional way. Apple products are portals to an amazing menu of continuing experiences that matter to a lot of us.

Over time, Michael Dell built a brilliantly designed computer manufacturing and delivery heavyweight. For a long time (by technology standards), Dell was the 800-pound gorilla in the space. Times change. Pretty soon, other makers mastered supply-chain management, which is now the price of admission. The PC itself was relegated to commodity status.

What to do?

Become brilliant at using design to provide an amazing customer experience.

That's what to do. This would be a reason why you care about design.

You know that design is on everyone's mind— it's almost a mantra. You see a new product—

a car, an iPod, or the latest cutting-edge cell phone—and you might think that a fairly straightforward process was involved in the product design. In some cases, this might be true, though often it's not. As a matter of fact, the process that delivers a good design—the physical embodiment of the product and how it looks and feels to a customer, which is so important for success—is often driven more by serendipity than by an integrated understanding of the design's impact on the broader idea of a product and business. Serendipity is a good thing—counting on it isn't.

We think most people are prone to define design, particularly good design, more narrowly than they should. When you see an iconic product, such as an iPhone, for instance, that enjoys an initial runaway success, it's so easy to overlook the big picture of how the product fits into the company's future—and the future of similar products in general. We want you to consider a far broader view of the significance of design.

Consider, for instance, the case of Motorola's Razr phone. Here is a product you might consider iconic. Historically, Motorola was an innovative company. The Razr has been a runaway success, although a bit of a fluke actually, because Motorola has never really understood what it had. Motorola just came up with a nice design and a nice form factor. The Razr was thin—designers sacrificed some footprint (height and width) for thinness. The design tied in with the naming, "Razr," and it worked, the imagery around the product struck a chord in people's hearts and minds. Motorola initially marketed the Razr well, but efforts since then have largely fallen flat.

Most people are prone to define design more narrowly than they should. We want you to consider a far broader view of the breadth and significance of design.

Motorola seemed to miss the point on the Razr. Instead of creating the next step in terms of the experience that people were resonating with, a mere veneer of the design was applied to subsequent products.

The design did not transform Motorola's culture. The company had only a single product, and now Motorola is back in trouble because it tried to repeatedly milk this one product over and over again. It hasn't worked. As we write this, Motorola is exploring spinning off its mobile devices unit "to recapture global market leadership and to enhance shareholder value." Whatever that means. It's a sad declaration, really. Martin Cooper invented the mobile cellular phone at Motorola. Remember "The Brick"? Then the Startac became an iconic product. Motorola could pioneer but could not build a design-driven culture to establish sustainable leadership. To be blunt, Motorola doesn't matter in the mobile market anymore.

This would be another reason you care about design.

Motorola tried to apply the veneer of the product to other products instead of saying, "What would be the next step in creating an experience that would resonate with people?" The company did not continue to grow, build on, and invest in what made the Razr successful. Instead, it chose to imitate, not innovate. Motorola repeatedly used the same language on different models and form factors. They added colors and used the same conventions, without life or soul. The company became stale almost overnight.

Motorola doesn't have a design culture. It has an engineering culture that tries to be a design culture. But the company fundamentally failed to see this. The product development folks seemed to say, "We'll make a cool thing, and that will be great," but they didn't develop the ability to consistently repeat it. On the operating system side, Motorola has never been able to design a great mobile phone user interface. The user experience suffers as a consequence. Design goes beyond simply the physical form factor. A big difference exists between a good design and a great product. Motorola didn't take the next steps to make the Razr the essential portal to people's mobile experience and hasn't been able to create consistent design cues across all customer touch points. Motorola might not even know that it matters—but it does.

You can create a good design, do it once and do it well, and have a nice object. That doesn't mean it will be a great product or a good business. It might be mildly successful, it might win some awards, and it might even get some buzz on the blogs. The difference between a great product and a merely good product, however, is that a great product embodies an idea that people can understand and learn about—an idea that grows in their minds, one they emotionally engage with.

The difference between a great product and a merely good product is that a great product embodies an idea that people can understand and learn about—an idea that grows in their minds, one they emotionally engage with.

Right now, you could design a product that looks like an iPhone, has really nice details and materials, and becomes an object of lust. However, this doesn't mean that it will ultimately be successful. Unless you have a strong idea that pervades the way it looks, the way it operates, what it does, how it's communicated to people, how it's branded, and how people identify with the brand, your product is not complete, because these are all things that go into making a great product which becomes a good business. Timing matters too. Until we started carrying mobile phones, digital cameras, a PDA, an MP3 player, and often a laptop, we would not have realized how much we wanted an iPhone that integrates much of this combined capability in a single compact and gorgeous device.

One of the core themes of this book is that design establishes the relationship between your company and your customers. So the complete design should incorporate what they see, interact with, and come in contact with—all the things they experience about your company and use to form opinions and to develop desire for your products. These touch points should not be allowed to just happen. They must be designed and coordinated in a way that gets you where you want to be with your customer—to where you matter to them. (And believe us, you want to matter.)

This approach is product design as a total concept—how the product operates, how it sounds, and how it feels. Included in the design is the experience of how you buy it, the experience of what happens when you actually get possession of it and open up the box, how you start to feel, and what all this communicates to you. And of course, there is the chain of events through which you became aware of the product. This is part of the design too—what all those touch points meant to you.

Taking possession of the product is just the beginning of the next phase of the relationship. What happens if something goes wrong with the product? What happens next? How do you feel about it? All these things need be included in the total design of the customer experience. This notion is something that IDEO (a Palo Alto design firm formed in 1991) has been basing its entire practice on—the idea that design is not just limited to this thing with buttons. This idea expands to designing all the interactions people have with the products that create (or destroy) the relationship people have with your company and determine whether you matter to them. Some of this is design in the old sense of creating visuals and materials, and some of it involves designing the total experience. For example, what should the telephone service experience be? How is that designed? Because it *is* designed—either consciously or by default.

The message here is this: Really grasp this idea of design—or you die. And, oh, yes—your products themselves have to be great.

Design or Die

For companies that make products (or provide services, for that matter), design or die is, in fact, the deal. Businesspeople must understand how to design the customer experience or be laid to rest in the graveyard of irrelevance. To an amazingly large degree, the American automotive industries don't seem to get design. Why? We don't have a satisfying answer to this question. But European car companies are consistently outperforming American car companies on the basis of design. We can guess that they haven't fully figured out how to focus on the experience they want to create and provide, which then impacts all that follows. The really sad thing is that when the U.S. auto industry was king, design was its mantra. Think bold chrome and fins. (Okay, maybe not cool now, but cool then.)

Here's another really important idea: When it's all said and done, your customer doesn't care about your process. To you, the logistics

When it's all said and done, your customer doesn't care about your process. In the end, none of this matters if the design experience is wrong.

of everything are important. The process of getting things engineered, getting them manufactured, analyzing the cost structures—all this is very important. Businesspeople love this stuff because it's Excel friendly and all very quantifiable. But in the end, none of this matters if the design experience is wrong. You can base all your boundary conditions on cost, timing, and market opportunity, and use the data to make a decision. Along the way, you'll likely throw out some ideas because they're too expensive or they'll take too long, so you'll end up with a mediocre product that no one buys. A perfect process doesn't matter unless the total design is right (ask Dell).

The question to ask is, "What is the design experience?" This is exactly what Apple does. It asks, "What design experience do we want? Let's do whatever it takes with our system to get it out the other end." For example, other people have tried to open stores where people can play with the products and then buy them. Gateway did it and wound up closing the stores. Dell is talking about playing with it. Of course, Dell won't be able to replicate the Apple experience because it doesn't have a design-driven culture yet.

The iPod is an iconic product of our time, a glorious example of design and business success. So close your eyes and imagine you're holding an iPod. Now take away iTunes, take away the ability to buy the song you like for 99¢ without having to pay $15 for a dozen more on a CD you don't want, lose the ability to create play lists, cut out the packaging, take out the ads, delete the Apple logo, and shutter all the Apple stores. The remaining question is, "Do you still have an

Courtesy of Apple Inc.

iPod?" Yes, the physical product in your hand is exactly the same, but what do you have now? Really, what do you have?

Well, you have a nicely designed object. Is it an iPod still? No, it's not, because an iPod is a portal to a kaleidoscope of experience. An iPod is not just an object. The object is an icon that is a portal to an experience.

Great products are about ideas; they are not just objects.

So this is a huge distinction that develops thematically throughout this book. *Successful* businesspeople in all fields endeavor to understand that they are in the business of designing a total customer experience. We call this *the customer experience supply chain.* The physical product or service is a central part—but, alone, not a sufficient part—of the equation for lasting success. Design is everyone's job. Doing good design takes more than good designers. It takes a commitment from *everybody* in the company—soup to nuts, end to end.

Of course, Apple is the obvious example of a company that understands the customer experience supply chain. In the automotive world, BMW is usually offered up as the icon because it definitely designs a great automobile; it's dedicated to designing the broader experience of owning a car and what that means to an individual owner. For example, we know that BMW spends a lot of time not just on the aesthetics and the materials, but on questions similar to these: How does it sound when you close the door? How does the steering wheel feel when you turn it? These questions are driven not just from a mechanic's point of view—how will we get the door to open?—but also from the customer's view when he or she grabs the handle and pushes the button. How does that feel? The customer closes the door, and it makes a sound. How does it sound? These are all design elements.

IKEA is another great example. Of course, IKEA uses design in its products and figured out how to make good design available at a low cost, but it's more than that. Design also applies to the nature of the store. Although IKEA has enjoyed substantial growth and now the experience isn't as good as it used to be, the core idea of building simple, well-designed, knock-down furniture and presenting it in this really amazing environment is still intact. It's not just "Here's the furniture, here's different ways you can use the furniture, and here's how you can ...." The idea includes virtually tutoring people on design and how they set up their homes to support a great experience of living at a very low cost. IKEA represents a great approach to product design and a really great approach to the design of the customer experience.

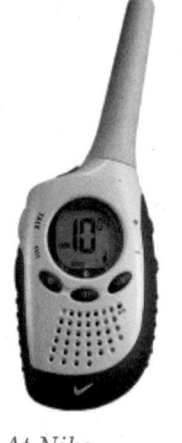

At Nike,
the product
experience
must always be
authentic to the
performance of
the sport, even
when the ultimate
customer is
not an athlete.

In the apparel industry, Nike got it and has kept getting it. Levi Strauss had it once and lost it—the tragic destruction of an iconic brand that is beyond comprehension.

At Nike, people stay intently focused on athletic authenticity. The vast majority of Nike customers aren't athletes. That said, Nike focuses on keeping its product design and brand very much in orbit around athletic performance. It's very aspirational. People who probably haven't jogged a quarter mile in five years wear Nike sweats and Nike shoes because it feels authentic. For these people, it's not just about apparel design; it's the design of the marketing message and the athletes they associate themselves with. "Tiger—you can't have his swing, but you can wear his clothes" proclaims a Niketown poster.

At Nike, the dialogue always goes way beyond "We're designing watches and walkie-talkies" to "What makes this product authentic to the performance of the sport?" The design must include this content, especially in the category definition phase of establishing the meaning of a product. After the category is defined, Nike focuses more on fashion, leverage, and how to build it out. But it starts with some seed of authenticity in the design.

Nike has always included its celebrity endorsements with the same kind of thoughtfulness. It ensures authenticity to athleticism in incorporating the celebrity messaging into its entire brand, the store, and the design of the Nike experience. This is another example of integrated design—of managing the total customer experience supply chain.

We need to define what we're talking about—what design means. So let's take a shot at this.

When you think about design, and particularly the category of industrial design, the temptation is to begin thinking about a physical object and not go much further. So let's go further and define design as the overt, thoughtful development of the interaction points between you and your customer. This definition includes the obvious interaction point of the thing that you touch, wear, eat, watch, listen to, or drive, and moves to a less obvious interaction point: the catalyst of all the emotions you experience when you interact with a company in some way.

If we boil down this idea to its point of intensity, effective design establishes the emotional relationship you develop with a brand through the total experience, to which a service or product provides a portal. (We are jumping ahead of ourselves here, implicitly raising the question posed in Chapter 2, "Do You Matter?," as a company, a brand, or a CEO.)

Effective design establishes the emotional relationship you develop with a brand through the total experience, to which a service or product provides a portal.

This question and the book title came from analyzing what defines a good brand. While teaching an engineering class at Stanford University about the emotional side of design, we asked, "Who cares if Motorola goes out of business next week?" One person raised his hand. We then asked, "Who cares if Apple goes out of business next week?" Most of the class raised their hands. If you are the CEO of Motorola, this is not good news because you were just told that you don't matter very much. If you don't think this is true, check your stock price.

Apple matters to people because it has designed aesthetically stunning hardware and a

If the answer to the question "Do you matter? comes back "no," this is not good news. If you don't think this is true, check your stock price.

total customer experience (think of this as software for the soul), so people feel connected to Apple in some deep emotional way. That's what great design does. It can make people love your company. In creating a broader definition of design, we include the emotions and feelings that arise to become part of the relationship people have with your company through every touch point that they experience. You don't want to let other people define this for you. If you're really smart about it, *you* define it. You can't entirely control it because people create their own version of the relationship, but you can commit to influencing this in every way you can. This is how you build an idea in people's mind of who you are as a company and as a brand.

We want to include in the meaning of design the "choreography of the experience" that people have of your company across whatever possible points of contact they can find.

We think this represents a shift, and it's what CEOs don't understand when they tell their people, "We've got to be design savvy."

It seems to us that you can't necessarily (or perhaps at all) understand what design means to a customer from just running a focus group. Our experience with customers is that many of them cannot articulate why they chose a particular product. They'll tell you why they *think* they chose it. But give somebody a Razr and an iPod, put them side by side, and ask, "Why don't you care if Motorola goes out of business, but you do care about iPod and Apple being around?" The answer to that question is what you need to hear and pay attention to. This is a clue to the question of the next chapter, "Do you matter?"

2

Do You Matter?

Who are you? What do you do? Why does it matter? Would the world be a darker place without you?

If someone took a poll today of your customers, constituents, followers, whatever, and asked if you matter to them, how do you think you would come out? If you ceased to exist tomorrow, do you think anyone would *really* care?

In other words, has your product, service, or brand established an emotional connection with your customers to the extent that they are invested in the interest that you not only survive, but also prosper?

In his book *The Brand Gap* (Peachpit Press, 2005), Marty Neumeier pitched this notion from a graphic design point of view. We would like you to consider the question in the context of a fully integrated definition of design.

Ask yourself questions such as "Who are you?" (which most people can answer) or "What do you do?" (you will probably get this one wrong). You might answer that you're a manufacturer of computers. Well, we say you're not merely a manufacturer of computers; you're creating systems to help people get work done. In light of this, why does what you do matter to people? Better yet, why do you matter at all?

This is the deep soul-searching question we want you to ask yourself. Does your company matter to your customers and constituents? Really, honestly, answer this. Are you a positive force in their lives? If you disappeared, would their lives be diminished in some way? I think if you tell yourself the truth, you might even conclude, "Well, probably not." Will we shed any tears if Cheer laundry detergent is not on the shelves anymore? No, probably not. Will we shed some tears if BMW suddenly ceased to exist? Yeah, we might. If Apple ceased to exist? Probably.

Why?

You matter to your customers to the degree that they become emotionally invested in your continuing success—when they want you to win.

This is an important question. You matter to your customers to the degree that they have become emotionally invested in your continuing success—when they want you to win. You matter if your customers believe in their bellies that their world would be a darker place without you. Using design to manage the customer experience supply chain is how you get to matter in this way that really counts.

Design is such a fundamental part of your life that we doubt that you go any stretch of time, even seconds, without bumping into something that has been designed. You might not be constantly aware of it, but we want to encourage this awareness.

People surround themselves with stuff and take its existence for granted. Every time you sit down on the toilet seat, somebody has designed that experience for you. Urban legend has it that, at one time, Herb Kohler personally had to sit on the prototype of every seat before he approved the design to go out the door. The point is that somebody has decided the shape, material, finish, angle, and height of the seat, and all these things define the start to your day. But we mostly take all this for granted and don't even think about it.

It's interesting—no, actually, it's fascinating—that most people really notice design only when it's bad. How many times do you hear someone say, "This fricking thing doesn't work; it's a pain in the butt." Really good design will many times be totally transparent to the user because "it just works." A design-savvy person will say, "Oh, this is really great design; it's making my life easier. Someone has really thought this through." Developing an awareness of excellent design as the connective tissue that defines and ensures an excellent experience for your customers is a vital key to the future of your business.

You have probably thought about design more than you realize. Surrounded by stuff, we've manufactured most of our world of experience without much use of conscious awareness. As you develop the level of design focus we're talking about here, we believe you will begin to move this understanding from your subconscious mind into active awareness. You will begin to witness design as an active part of any experience, good or bad. You might even, as a business person, categorically dislike dealing with designers, but at least develop a love of knowing what the deal about design is.

By way of example, let's say after a lovely flight from London in Virgin Atlantic's Upper Class, you find yourself in the Washington–Dulles

Design is such a fundamental part of our lives that we cannot go seconds without having an experience defined for us.

airport going through immigration. Having just been informed that if you fire up your mobile phone it will be summarily confiscated, you now notice it's a total bottleneck at both ends of the facility. Everybody coming in one end is compacted into a tiny space, and then after being processed, people spill out into a second tiny space. As you stand there, you can hear those who have the energy left to be vocal proclaiming that the system basically sucks, and it requires no psychic ability on your part to figure out that folks feel abused and angry (and this is the capital of the United States).

As a design-aware person, you start to think about how wretchedly designed the system is. Somewhere, some group of architects completely failed to grasp their impact on a traveler's experience when they laid out the labyrinth. The result is a design failure at work. If this was your company showroom or your store, and people had this bad experience getting into it because you hadn't designed it thoughtfully, it would cost you money. If the Apple store had a dysfunctional layout and no one could see the products or play with them, people would walk out of the store going, "Forget Apple, I won't buy their stuff."

In reality, a visit to the Apple Store at 767 Fifth Avenue in New York City is a shining example of a totally designed customer experience.

As awareness of good design grows, we believe that people actually care more about design than they realize. At the same time, we see that people leading organizations are beginning to understand that the quality of a customer's experiences is the essential element of continuing success. However, grasping this and successfully implementing a wildly effective customer experience design strategy are two entirely different things.

In complete contrast to the Washington–Dulles travel experience, if you happen to travel to Dubai, it will be hard for you to ignore the majestic Burj Al Arab Hotel. People thought Sheik Mohammed was crazy when he built this. He reportedly spent $2 billion, a sum approaching 20% of the country's gross national product (GNP) at that time. It's an amazing icon and has come to symbolize Dubai, creating a message that anything is possible. Rooms start at $1,700 a night, and the place is booked for months in advance. Think about the power of design here, because they designed this experience and this shape. When you Google Dubai, you'll probably see a picture of the hotel, you'll know it, recognize it, and respond to it as an icon for opulence and luxury.

At the inception of the project, it was easy for a rational mind to think they were crazy, building this hotel out on that sandbar and creating this really interesting but challenging and expensive-to-build shape. You could easily ask, "Why are you spending this money?" You can see the payoff now: Because it's so iconic and has such draw, they can charge $1,700 a night and be booked up for months. This is a stunning example of experience supply chain design, in which you use design also as a marketing strategy. The design is so powerful that you don't need to spend as much on marketing because the design is already doing marketing for you.

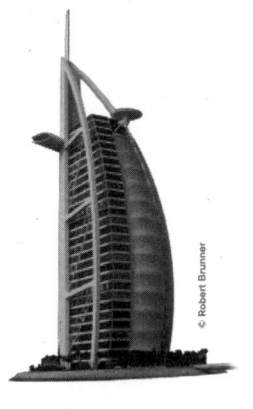

The Burj Al Arab Hotel in Dubai is a stunning example of experience design in which the design itself is the marketing strategy.

Industrial design is usually seen as the development of objects for mass production, typically three dimensional, physical objects. We're advocating a concept of product design that incorporates far more.

We want you to think again about design itself, with a renewed emphasis on an integrated design strategy—creating the total customer experience. What we're talking about goes beyond industrial design, which conjures up images of factories, piping systems, and so on. Industrial design is essentially the development of objects for mass production, typically three-dimensional, physical objects or the interaction with them. Current training focuses on this type of design. We're advocating a concept of product design that incorporates far more. The major disciplines of design are industrial design, graphic design, and architecture. You can start to make distinctions within these categories, such as interior architecture, landscape architecture, traditional building construction, and so forth. Product design, as we discuss it, occupies a gray area between industrial design (the design of physical objects and the associated interactions) and software design. A lot of overlap exists between those two areas, and out of that overlap, the idea of interaction design has really emerged as its own discipline.

Now, here's the really important thing to note about interaction design: It needs to matter to you, *but to your customer, it doesn't matter,* because good interaction is natural and should be totally transparent. Customers also don't care about which disciplines were involved and who did what. They don't really discern among the contributions of the industrial designer, the graphic designer, and the architect—to them, it's what they feel that matters. Their desired experience is emotional, one that lives mostly just below the threshold of consciousness instead of in total awareness. You matter to customers only to the extent that you have become associated with this desired part of their lives.

Automobiles are a part of our lives for which we more actively think about design, way beyond just where they put the beverage holders. The Lexus division of the Toyota Motor Corporation redefined the customer experience in the luxury auto market. The quality of the experience became the luxury, and the other luxury brands scrambled to catch up. But nothing lasts forever if you fall asleep at the wheel.

Let's say you're a certified tree-hugger and decide to join the wave and get a hybrid. You look around and land on the Lexus Rx400h, the SUV hybrid (you need an SUV because you've got enough stuff to start your own world), which, from a technology point of view, looks like a fantastic car. So this seems like a good idea at the time. You take delivery and rapidly learn that the gas mileage is not what you were promised. Whenever you use the car, you have to use a touch-screen interface, not just for the navigation system, but for everything. It's unbelievably badly designed, to the point you decide it's dangerous.

You matter to customers only to the extent that you have become connected to their emotional needs and desires.

The GPS navigation system's user interface is insane. If you don't use it every day, you have no chance of remembering how to use it the next time you really need it. And, of course, you can't modify your route or your destination while the vehicle is in motion, and you conclude that stopping in the middle of a freeway to do so might be injurious to your health.

Because of your bad experience with the car's user interface and the less-than-promised gas economy, and despite brilliant mechanical engineering and terrific acceleration, this vehicle becomes the least satisfying car you have ever owned. You might be a pretty technologically savvy individual, but you decide to trade cars again because it's such a bad experience (read: design failure here). You spend too much time in your car to endure constant irritation. You paid a premium for a Lexus and a premium for a hybrid, all for the promise of a better experience. But the design is so poor when viewed from the owner's total experience that your expectations have been betrayed. The failure is ridiculous because Lexus could easily have acquired the needed expertise to design the user interface really well.

And here's where the experience goes from bad to ugly. You write to the Lexus division of the Toyota Motor Company to share your experience. You receive four surveys, two calls, and a couple e-mails—all because the company wants to tap your experience to improve its future. The inquiries are not about you and correcting your problem; it is about making the company's business better. No solutions are offered to you. So how does all this feel? Having fun yet? You vow never to buy a Lexus vehicle again. The Toyota Motor Corporation no longer matters to you except in a negative way. By now you want them to lose. And do you keep these sentiments to yourself? No, probably not. You might even invent a new game called "How many sales can I cost them?"

So you buy another vehicle and you pass on the built-in navigation system. For navigation, you get yourself a Garmin Nüvi GPS device. It doesn't even come with an instruction manual. If you want an instruction manual, you need to access the Garmin web site and download it.

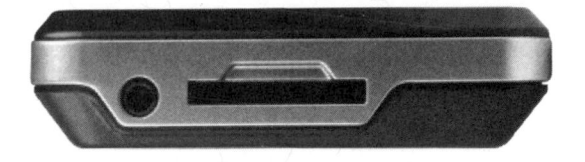

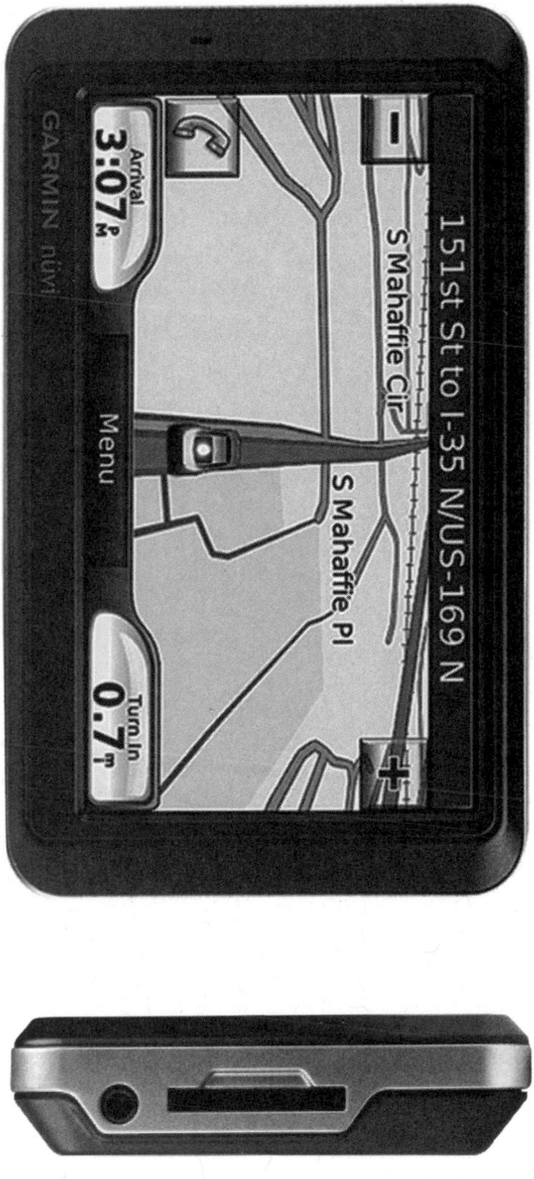

The Nuvi comes with a quick-start guide, which doesn't really give you much in the way of information. It tells you how to charge it, turn it on, and do a few other basics to get you going. But anybody you give it to can use it to navigate with no instructions other than onscreen prompts and the intuitive design. At this point, it's beyond you why organizations such as Lexus wouldn't outsource their user interface design to a company such as Garmin.

You have to get beyond usability for great design. It has to be desirable too.

Time to change hats again. If you're an entrepreneur, a product manager, or a CEO reading this, ask yourself, "Do we really matter to our customers?" If you are honest with yourself, you might say, "Here's where maybe we matter, and here's where maybe we don't." This isn't an inquiry you can or should shrug off. It's as vital to your survival as oxygen. Are you connecting with customers on an emotional level? Are you even seeing the whole picture and getting accurate feedback on the customer experience without inconveniencing them with your data collection process? Do your customers care if you live or die? You definitely want that answer to be "Yes."

It doesn't matter what product, service, or brand you think about. Do you really value and honor the experience of your customers with a design that encompasses every aspect of the way you do business? Let's see how this can play out when service is a big part of the equation.

Consider, for example, the couple that has been a loyal GEICO customer for years. The two have perfect driving records, and every time a cute commercial airs with a lovable lizard pitching how warm and fuzzy the company is, they nod at each other and smile, "That's our company." Then they move and make their change of address on the GEICO web site. However, the mail goes to their former address, so it's delayed in reaching them. They send a check the same day they receive their bill. But before the company processes the check, they receive a letter announcing "NOTIFICATION OF POLICY CANCELLATION." That rockets them out of their matching recliners. They call the company 800-number and are calmed down by a customer service rep who tells them not to worry, that he will call the moment their check clears the system. However, while they wait

Virtually any emotional pebble in the customer's road can become magnified into a perceptual paradigm shift resulting in negative feelings about your company.

to hear from him, they get an e-mail with the subject heading "NOTIFICATION OF POLICY CANCELLATION." They send a "shame on you" e-mail back to GEICO, and then they receive a form-letter note of contrition. When the customer service rep calls to tell them all is well, they say, "No, it isn't." They have now been motivated to shop around; in a few days, they get a better deal from Progressive for the same coverage, and they cancel the policy they carried with GEICO for years.

There you have it. An emotional pebble in the road has resulted in a paradigm shift in which customers who felt good about their experience with a company (or, at least, not negative) did a total flip-flop. Now every time a GEICO commercial airs, they fantasize about strangling that bloody lizard. The commercials are designed to demonstrate that it, as a company, cares about you. But to the couple, all the company really seemed to care about was the money. No doubt a meeting occurred somewhere in the insurance company's halls in which someone proposed that the company put a bit more teeth in its mailings to late payers; that person might never have realized that he or she was part of a design process that would ultimately impact whether customers cared if the company lived or died.

Now it's about you wearing your entrepreneurial, product manager, or CEO hat again. How's it going with your company? Do you matter? Go back to asking yourself the tough questions, and "unto thine own self be true" with the answers:

- Do your customers care if you're around tomorrow?

- What kind of product loyalty do your customers have?

- Does your product experience make a positive emotional connection with your customers?

- Does your product or brand add value to people's lives?

- Does everyone in your company realize to what extent they play a part in the total experience design?

- Do your customers come back because they want to or because they have to?

- Are they on the verge of a very Schwarzenegger-like, "Hasta la vista, baby" if a competitor or impetus to change comes along?

- Are you a valued friend to your customer?

The fine point we want you to grasp is that just having a connection is one thing; ensuring that it is positive and remains so is another thing. If you look at a company such as Microsoft, it obviously has an emotional connection with customers. The company matters in the sense that, to a lot of people in the world, if Microsoft shut down tomorrow, many people would be up a creek without a paddle when it comes to getting work done. But on the emotional side, is this connection energetically positive?

The existence of Microsoft is critical in people's business lives. But on the emotional side, is this connection energetically positive?

When Microsoft went out and talked to people about Windows so that it could really understand how its customers felt about the company, it found that most people thought about Windows and Microsoft in the same light as they think about the utility company, the phone company, or the water district. This might come as no surprise to you, but it was a big jolt to them: "They're a necessity, but I don't necessarily like them." You probably don't like your utility or cable company very much—especially your cable company. But what else can you do? You want cable. You need a computer and have to work in the Microsoft Office world, so what else can you do?

Microsoft was now aware of how a lot of people felt, namely that "If a real, credible alternative was offered, I'd switch." Awareness is not everything, however. If your company has a culture that is consensus driven, you might find more internal roadblocks and log jams than understanding and willingness to pitch in and participate in designing a positive customer experience. That's why it's so vital for the buy-in to this all-encompassing concept to come from high up in the company—it must come from the top, or near top, and include a critical mass of aspirational members of the organization. Sometimes the transformation begins with the aspirational members who engage the senior team as advocates and champions of the cause.

When a particular track is established, big companies, in particular, have an even harder time changing, even if they "know" they need to change. Although this can become difficult, establishing the right and thorough design track is so important because you can't revisit it as much as you might like. Changing direction is not always cost-effective, pragmatic, or even possible. Yet it's something so vital to your company that it needs constant supervision. Catch-22? Well, let's explore that.

If you have a direct relationship with your customer that doesn't require the customer's live involvement with your people, that's very valuable from an economic point of view. One terrifying and real thing for companies such as Dell is that the minute they have to get a person involved with the customer, they lose all the profit on many products. Because the margins have become so thin and the volume so high, profit on that product is usually lost as soon as they have to answer a sales call or a service call. On a high-volume product, you might be making only $10 of profit. The expense of the equipment and employee to answer the call can easily exceed $10, which eliminates your profit.

Creating a direct relationship with your customer that does not require live involvement with your people is very valuable from an economic point of view. Great design can give you this.

Any company working with scale can verify this. Banks learned long ago that they often lose money on transactions that involve human interaction. And how do you resonate with your customers at an emotional level without excessive human interaction? You design it in. If you create a positive relationship between the product and the end user, you don't have the expense of someone needing to explain, "Here's why this is important, this is how you use it, and this is why it matters to you."

Some companies, such as Apple, have designed into the equation the feeling that you have the support of a live person if and when you need it. If you buy a Mac, you can pay $100 for 12 months of live support by appointment. And even if you don't use it much or go into an Apple store that often, it's a heck of a deal— for just $100, you can go once a week to a live person (a.k.a. a Mac Genius) who will teach you how to use your Mac and core applications to create items of interest to you. And you're doing all this in a vibrantly designed Apple store buzzing with good vibes instead of some dingy classroom.

So you're sitting there getting one-on-one attention from some user-friendly person who really does know how it all works, surrounded by goodies you want that you add to your wish list. As they say, "How cool is that?" Way cool—especially for Apple. Because on the way out, you buy a wall charger for your iPod for $29.95. And even if you know you can get a DVD player for less than that at Best Buy, it doesn't seem to bother you. You have even forgiven Jobs for dropping the price of the iPhone by $200 after you had waited in line for hours and paid the original price to be an early adopter. Hmm, let's see—I guess, by now, Apple matters to you so much that sometimes you'll pay a premium for a continuing connection to the experience.

If you've been paying attention, you might figure out by now that this is the reason Apple's market cap is (as we write this) approximately half that of Microsoft. And Apple's market share of the U.S. personal computer market (and the operating system market) for the third calendar quarter of 2007 was only 8.1 percent. And if you

use a Mac, you probably use Microsoft Office, so
Microsoft still owns this market share. Yes, you
care about building a design-driven company.
You really want to matter to your customers.
You really do want them to want you to live long
and prosper.

How To Matter

*What design can do for you—how design
communicates with people—how the design of
products and services creates an emotional
connection with your customers—how great
design builds bulletproof brands.*

In the 1880s, Lunsford Richardson, a pharmacist
in Selma, North Carolina, was experimenting
with a formula to relieve colds and pneumonia for
his customers. He arrived at the active ingredients of Camphor, Eucalyptol, and menthol, and
inactive ingredients of cedar leaf oil, nutmeg oil,
Petrolatum, Thymol, and turpentine oil. A classic was born. The product succeeded because it
worked when other products sold by snake oil
salesmen didn't. People came to depend on it, and
they liked it better than anything else they had
tried. Richardson moved to Greensboro, North
Carolina, and started marketing his formula as
Vicks VapoRub, in honor of his brother-in-law,
a Selma physician named Dr. Joshua Vick.

  The company become known as the Vicks
Chemical Company and was sold to Procter &
Gamble (P&G) in 1985. VapoRub is currently
manufactured in Mexico and India. Why does it
keep selling? When people feel sick, they reach
for Vicks because it has formed an emotional
bond with a customer base that nothing has

The P&G Swiffer is an example of creating a connection that extends beyond its function and into the joy of use.

replaced. VapoRub's brand value seems pretty bulletproof even today. What would happen if P&G tried to take Vicks off the market? Public outrage. People care. The product matters.

Product design enlightened by the customer experience has been around for some time. Although the packaging for Vicks VapoRub is unlikely to end up on permanent display at a museum of packaging art, the product continues to be mindfully marketed by P&G, who is really good at brand management. A focus to deeply connect with the customer has become increasingly important as the organizing principle of a total design. And we think this will always be the case—not just for success, but for survival. Your design, brand, business, and company must matter in the heart and mind of your customer.

When P&G released the Swiffer in 1999, it caught on—not because it mimicked design cues that could make it the iMop, but because it made life easier for anyone cleaning a floor or spill. People liked that. The bond was emotional. No more of the distasteful wringing out a mop and then deciding where to hang it while it dried. Just throw away the pad. Someone thought about the parts of daily life that aren't easy or fun and found a way around them. That made people happy. That's what drives modern product performance, as with any traditional product that has survived. People connect with it and buy it. They justify purchase decisions with reason and stay connected through emotion. You must continually contemplate how engaging hearts and minds is part of your total concept of product design.

Notice that we did not start out this chapter with examples of design that were stunning physical objects destined to become objects of lust, such as the iPhone. This would only have reinforced an already too limited concept of design implanted in too many minds. Yes, you can become a choreographer of timeless objective beauty, if you want. However, if this is all you are, it won't be enough. You don't start with all the stuff you have in the back end or all the stuff you have on the shelf; you start with a person who is, or will become, your enduring customer. And you should ask yourself, "What do I want that person to feel?" What do I want my customer to feel after he has bought my plasma screen? If you've ever arrived home with a wagonload of home theater gear and tried to hook up an HDTV monitor, a receiver, and a 5.1 surround system, you've definitely wished someone had asked this question sometime during the design process.

When Best Buy couldn't get manufacturers to collaboratively work this out, and they knew it was costing them money, they bought The Geek Squad, who will show up in their VW Bugs and (for a fee) get it together for you. The consumer electronics industry desperately needs to listen and apply the Apple tag line: "it just works." In the meantime, get yourself a Logitech Harmony Remote if you're desperately seeking home theater domestic harmony. You'll have a direct experience of what great design can do for you. Harmony felt customers' pain as they struggled with an array of miserably designed remotes and on-screen user interfaces that even an engineer's mother couldn't love. Then Harmony developed an activity-based design for its universal remote. People and the reviewing press love them.

When Best Buy could not get manufacturers to work out the complexity of setting up their products, they bought the Geek Squad to help remedy the situation.

Often, great product successes do not start out scripted and defined. You start with an idea, you see something working, you develop it, and you run with it.

That's what good design is about. So when you're creating a product, what do you want people to feel when they take delivery? When they use it? The product and its impact can be growing and evolving. Quite often, great successes do not start out scripted and designed. You have an idea, you start somewhere, you see something working, you develop it, and you run with it. You hit snags; you iron them out. It's simultaneously a conscious and strategic process.

Let's take a look at the iPod as an example of how you can design and evolve a product. We want you to pay special attention to how the process of creating a customer experience supply chain did not flow from a set script and was certainly not without snags and obstacles. Look from a 40,000-foot level and see that after Apple had embraced the idea of the iPod as a portal to a rich user experience, it kept running with it, building on it, making it better, and looking for more opportunities. In *Success Built to Last* (Plume, 2007), authors Porras, Emery, and Thompson describe the unexpected role of serendipity in the journey to greatness. This is certainly true in the story that follows.

First, consider the recorded music environment from a customer perspective in those pre-iPod days. With the advent of CDs, the 45-rpm single was dead. Now if you wanted to buy a single song you liked, you had to buy a whole CD for $15 to $20 to get the one song you wanted, plus a dozen more you didn't give a damn about. Screw Big Music is pretty much how you felt about that if you were a teenager or a college student. Then along came Napster, Kaaza, and the file-sharing universe. During the ongoing legal war between Big Music and its customer base, the idea that you should be able to buy a single cut from a CD penetrated the mainstream. Still, although you could now legally load songs onto a hard drive, this fell far short of a pinnacle of portable convenience.

The iPod story has been told in a number of places and in multiple versions. While we share with you our version (although not Apple approved), we want you to focus on the aspects of the underlying design process that will help you develop products and services that matter. Also think about the implications of the fact that *Apple did not invent what became the iPod.* Instead, Apple developed (and this is what matters) the iPod as a portal to an incredibly valuable ongoing consumer experience—a huge distinction.

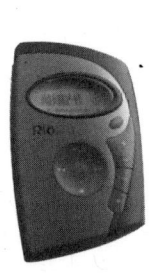

Our story starts with Tony Fadell, who had worked for General Magic and Philips and set himself up as an independent contractor because he had an idea he wanted to shop around.[1] Bulky flash memory–based MP3 players were on the market from companies such as Rio, or the Nomad Jukebox (from Singapore-based Creative). The Nomad was about the size of a CD player, and it had a hard disk in it. It was phenomenal, in the sense that suddenly you could load your whole collection of music on this one piece of hardware and begin to understand the power of a digital music device.

Apple did not invent what became the iPod. Instead, Apple developed the iPod as a portal to an incredibly valuable ongoing consumer experience.

Of course, there was a list of "buts." The Nomad had a really miserable user interface that most people barely understood, and its battery life was abysmal. You couldn't really use it as a portable unit; it was best suited for a home stereo. And you could create play lists, but only with some difficultly. At 6 inches in diameter by about 1.5 inches thick, you could put it in your backpack, but you probably wouldn't carry it around. Fadell wanted to deliver a small hard drive–based player linked to a content delivery system through which users could legally download music and easily create playlists. "A 1,000 songs in your pocket" was the idea here. People loved it. Good start. He was on the path to an emotional link with customers, but he had a ways to go.

Fadell shopped his idea to companies such as RealNetworks, Philips, and Palm. When they said no (consider the irony of this: Palm was on a roll at the time, and now it's teetering on the edge of a hungry grave), he reluctantly approached Apple, knowing the company was consumer electronics shy after painful experiences with the Pippin and Newton. He didn't know Apple had bought the rights to SoundJam MP a few months before he approached the company. Apple hired Fadell in 2001 and gave him a team of about 30 people and a one-year deadline to build out and release a product.

With limited time and uncertain funding, Fadell looked around for an existing player to use as a basis for the Apple player. After looking at Rio and Creative, his team found PortalPlayer, which had not yet released its own player, although it had helped other companies develop MP3 players using common software. Before Apple, PortalPlayer had been working with IBM on a flash memory–based player with a Bluetooth headphone system, but it thought its chances of getting to a consumer-friendly MP3 player would be better by working with Apple.

According to Ben Knauss, who was at that time a senior manager for PortalPlayer, Fadell was filled with optimism and predicted from the start, "This is the project that's going to remold Apple, and ten years from now, it's going to be a music business, not a computer business." But the first PortalPlayer prototypes could not handle a play list larger than ten songs, did not have equalizers, and had outdated interfaces. On top of that, the player's batteries lasted for less than three hours. And as Knauss has admitted, "It was fairly ugly. It looked similar to an FM radio with a bunch of buttons."

PortalPlayer's reference design was 80-percent complete when Apple came along. The company dropped a dozen other clients to work exclusively with Apple. For Apple and its tight schedule, the attraction was that the software and hardware were already done. According to Knauss, Apple spent eight months using the company's 200 American employees and 80 engineers in India to focus exclusively on the design and development of the iPod. Even more important to the project's success, Steve Jobs became personally involved in the project, eventually giving it nearly all his time — something he rarely did.

Initially, Jobs's involvement was in iPod meetings every two or three weeks. But as soon as the first prototypes were completed, he got involved on a daily basis. From Fadell's notion and business plan, Jobs's participation meant approaching the project from the customer's point of view and using that perspective to mold the device's shape, feel, and design. Jobs reportedly threw a fit if he couldn't get to a song in three touches of a button. "We'd get orders," said Knauss. "Steve doesn't think it's loud enough, the sharps aren't sharp enough, or the menu's not coming up fast enough." He focused on every detail, from the interface to the size of the scroll wheel. Even Jobs's quirks show through. The iPod ended up louder than most other MP3 players.

In spite of all the hard work, and a good deal of typical Apple obsessive secrecy during the design process, the product nearly died just before it was scheduled to ship. It drained batteries even when turned off. It could run for maybe three hours, and then it just died. With production lines already set up, the mad scramble that took place to fix the problem and ship the product is a CEO's nightmare.

When the first iPod finally did roll out, inside was a 5GB Toshiba hard drive about the size of a quarter, the same ARM processor used in the Newton and the Acorn, an operating system from Pixo, a large high-resolution display, a lithium polymer battery (that could last quite a bit longer than three hours), and, of course, the scroll wheel.[2] This was a distinct departure from the Sony Walkman kind of controls, a huge advantage for the user who could now simply spin a wheel to sort through a capacity for thousands of songs. This feature gave the iPod a significant experiential user advantage over MP3 players such as those from Nomad or Compaq. One profound lesson here is that details matter big-time. Jobs knew this and got involved at the level of tiniest design detail to make the iPod a success.

In a way, the iPod story is a dream scenario for what we are discussing here. Design, as a fully integrated approach to the user experience, contains elements of risk, serendipity, and lessons learned from failure. As with anything in life, you don't get anywhere by sitting comfortably in your living room, warm and cozy. You really have to step outside and take risks to make progress. This is an important part of design as well—after you learn from your failures and you get on to something that's working, you build on it and move forward. Behind all the scrambling and luck—sometimes good, sometimes bad—you see a consciously designed series of events emerge in which you earn your good fortune by being incredibly intentional about creating an experience with great design as a core strategic element.

Apple has released subsequent generations and versions of the iPod. The premiere version was presented to the world in a rented auditorium in Cupertino to a shocked audience that was more hostile than friendly. The $400 price and absence of Windows compatibility were considered two strikes against the first iPod. Although the reception in Europe was more enthusiastic, Apple was quick to roll out a 10GB version and, as soon as it could, provide a utility that enabled users to access the iPod experience from a Windows PC. As part of the evolutionary process, Apple replaced the original spinning scroll wheel with a solid-state version, similar to a notebook touchpad. And the beat went

Design, as a fully integrated approach to the user experience, contains elements of risk, serendipity, and lessons learned from failure.

on, through generations two, three, four, and beyond. The driving principle of each change and iteration came from an intense focus on the customer experience, by valuing customers' emotional connection to the Apple-enabled world of digital music.

The iPod is an iconic product, a portal to a customer experience that has redefined an entire industry. Jobs did not play the game; he changed the game.

The crucial point of the evolving iPod story is that if you want to transform your brand to the point where you matter, you have to start with design that's "designed in" not "added on." It can't be a veneer. Design is not an event or a process you apply to physical and mechanical reality. You are designing a customer experience supply chain. If you are the CEO and this is something you really want to do, it's not just a matter of getting together your executive staff and saying, "Go design some good stuff." You have to look at your business from beginning to end and see how it all relates to your customer; then you must decide how you will design all the pieces of a customer experience solar system and go about accomplishing true organizational change.

You won't accomplish this by holding an offsite meeting and saying, "And remember that design's important these days, so report back to me in six months and show me some really cool stuff." You have to design an entire organizational system aligned top to bottom with being design driven. Any dissonance in the culture design, the organizational structure, and the incentives will produce toxic waste in the

If you want to transform your brand to the point where you matter, you have to start with design that is "designed in" not "added on"

environment and you will lose. Trust us on this—the environment always wins.

Let's loop back to Jobs and Apple for a moment. Was the reception to the idea of what became the iPod, and all the steps that followed, mostly luck (remember, some capable companies passed), or was it the result of a company-wide driving spirit of regard for the "customer experience" embedded in the Apple culture? Our answer is that "you earn your luck." Take the Macintosh as an example. It might have started with a belief in the power of the personal computer, but the good design started with seeking to bring this power to the people in a form factor they could use. The process that led to the Mac evolved through the development of the Apple I and II, Apple's focus on releasing reasonably priced, reliable, and easy-to-use computers for the rest of us.

You probably recall that the early Apples didn't look appealing, and the message wasn't great. However, the ease of use and what happened on the screen from a user experience made the Mac an icon. The company figured out the power of design, and Jobs drove that from many points of view—from the size, to the insistence on an elegant graphic user interface for the operating system, to the incorporation of a mouse, to the insistence that it couldn't have a fan. He wanted the total experience to be great. You must get the experience right. Jobs and Apple transformed the computer from this sort of complicated, scientific thing into this cute little box—one with killer applications such as Adobe Photoshop and PageMaker.

Being design driven won't be accomplished by holding an offsite meeting and saying "design is important, so report back in six months with some cool stuff."

That was the first period for Apple. The second period began when the company understood the power of the icon and the physical experience. During the first period, the company used what we refer to in design language as "Silicon Valley provincial." It was from the HP genre—everything was beige, contained angles on the corners, and was designed like a credenza. Then Apple said, "Look, there's a whole other world out there." And that's when Jobs hired Hartmut Esslinger and Frog Design to create what was one of the first and most successful brand-driven design languages—driving toward a look and feel that will be pervasive across a product line (design language is the subject of Chapter 7, "Your Products and Services Are Talking to People"). They were very successful at that. This was when design took hold and Apple became a bona fide design-driven enterprise.

The period between after Jobs was fired and before he was encouraged to return was about leveraging the impact of being a design-driven enterprise and growing it. People don't realize that although this period is somewhat forgotten, Apple grew into a $12 billion company and was selling products everywhere. It really leveraged the idea of the Apple brand. At the same time, the flurry of activities focused toward growth shifted some of the tightness of focus away from the total customer experience. John Scully was a good leader, with design in his background (Rhode Island School of Design), and he had a strong interest in innovation (such as the original PowerBook), but at the same time many people were coming in from Sun and HP, and the company goal was to make the business big and broad. Apple continued to build an extraordinary design capacity, make great products, and win awards, but all the various parts of the business side were trying to be everything for everyone, which diminished the focus on core Apple experience and ideals.

You don't sacrifice the experience for growth; you drive growth from the quality of the experience.

Then Jobs came back and refocused on creating a significantly better user experience. He said, "Look, this is about the experience, and you have to understand that the most powerful asset that Apple has is its brand and the experience that people have. You cannot sacrifice that. In fact, you have to constantly make it better." That ushered in the third period, and with it, the iMac. If you look back, Apple has always been about icons. It had the PowerBook, which still stands today as the MacBook—the same design with different materials. It had the original Mac, then the iMac, and then the iPod, and now the iPhone, the Apple TV, and the MacBook Air. These products have always represented the company's core values. It's interesting design history, but Apple didn't have it from the very beginning. It has been a living, growing process. The Mac illuminated the power of experience design and the iconic nature of products similar to it.

The possibility for an organization to get the notion of "Don't just play the game, change the game" goes far beyond the world of electronic devices and household products. No matter what business you're in, you should focus on this sort of integrated design. Let's look at an example from an entirely different category.

Cirque du Soleil (French for "Circus of the Sun") began in 1984 in Quebec with a synthesis of circus styles, no ring, no animals, no curtains, continuous live music, and a poetic central theme and storyline to its performances. During its 1988 North American tour, which included appearances at the Calgary Winter Olympics and in San Francisco, New York, Washington, and Toronto, it was a smashing iconic success. The title of the tour was "We Reinvent the Circus." But why did Cirque du Soleil feel the need to reinvent the circus?

In the heyday of the traveling circus, from 1880 to 1920, Barnum and Bailey's "The Greatest Show on Earth," the Ringling Brothers, and many more circuses such as these traveled in tent shows to all the major U.S. cities with clowns, elephants, acrobats, and a predictable array of apparitions, acts, and novelties. The circus, as an art or entertainment form, significantly declined in popularity during the 1950s and 1960s—a period infused with an increased concern for the welfare of animals and a general public boredom with a genre that had changed little in a world that was changing a lot. The circus was also a populist medium in a setting where it had to compete with television and a growing number of equally colorful distractions. Yet the circus drum beat on to an unchanged cadence, and the man was fired out of the cannon in the same way he had always been. It was no longer an emotionally moving experience for many people.

A Cirque du Soleil show is an unfolding, compelling story. It is a totally engaging experience that lifts the emotions. This is core to the whole concept.

Cirque du Soleil changed the game forever with an artful, integrated experience in a changing and evolving format, to become named *cirque nouveau*, the new circus. The audience also changed to one that appreciates skilled artisans swinging from sweeping drapes to music written by modern composers, amazing paired contortionists, and teams of acrobats working in synchronization—all to an unfolding, compelling story. It is a totally engaging experience that lifts the emotions and provides fresh entertainment.

Cirque du Soleil is now an annually touring business with movies, related products, and a yearly revenue of more than $500 million. P. T.

Barnum is likely spinning in his grave. However, its origins were more humble. Two street performers, Guy Laliberté and Daniel Gauthier, founded the company in 1984. The early years were tough, and they needed the support of government grants for two years. They hired Guy Caron away from The National Circus School to create the experience-driven atmosphere of shows with a central theme and storylines. The troupe had successes in the 1980s, such as the Los Angeles Arts Festival, but it also had failures. Then, under the direction of Franco Dragone, the show *Nouvelle Expérience* was created, and that brought Cirque profit by 1990 and encouraged new shows. But the driving and shaping force that ebbed and flowed and kept the show alive was a design based on experience, on an emotional engagement with the audience.

Janice Steinburg, who witnessed Cirque du Soleil's 1987 appearance in San Diego on its first American tour, said, "Like a really fabulous first kiss, that show lingers — it shimmers and dances in the memory of anyone who was lucky enough to experience it."[3] According to Mindy Donner, a puppeteer and arts educator, in the show that took place in a 1,500-seat tent in the parking lot of the former Naval Hospital near Balboa Park, there were "poignant characters on risky business, alone and vulnerable in the spotlight, or appearing and disappearing through fog and rigging." Reviewing for the *San Diego Tribune*, Robert J. Hawkins described the production *We Reinvent the Circus* as a "diaphanous illusion in which the ragtag artists stumbled out of the eerie light and mist ... clinging to each other like gentle escapees from some asylum." Said Steinburg, "I remember seeing those macabre, tender figures and being moved to tears."

We earlier mentioned that design, as a fully integrated approach to the user experience, contains elements of risk, serendipity, and lessons learned from failure. Few examples speak better to that than Cirque du Soleil. Laliberté not only reinvented the circus, but he also kept reinventing Cirque du Soleil, a process that continues as the company marches on. However, in the beginning, think of the courage it took to say, "Circuses are largely for children; we'll make it largely an adult experience. Circuses always have animals; we'll have no animals. Circuses show the same events wherever they go; we'll innovate a different event each time, and begin each with a story. Circuses offer a low form of entertainment; we'll raise it to a high form. Going to the circus is a cheap date; we'll raise the price point until the experience is aspirational, one that fewer can afford."

Laliberté sinks as much as 70 percent of the company's revenues into research and development for new themes and talent—quite a far cry from the 1987 show at the Los Angeles Arts Festival where the gamble was a huge risk. If the show had not been a success, Laliberté wouldn't have had the money to get the company and equipment back to Canada. Yet they did make it back and have achieved many successes in the face of a number of imitators. Cirque du Soleil accomplishes this by constantly reinventing itself and shifting designers and talent. It doesn't seek traditionally trained talent because these performers tend not to be independent thinkers—and that's the sort of verve this company wants to maintain.

With its enormous success, many are concerned that the growing commercialization will cause the Cirque to lose the magic that made it work in the first place. Is it possible to become overpolished and lose the humanity that made the emotional connection to its audience? Christopher Isherwood, in a *New York Times* review of Cirque's *KÁ* show at MGM Grand, said, "The sheer scope of this theatrical enterprise...precludes emotional engagement in the fate of the characters." Is it possible to offer the personal experience of the original shows yet have major audience appeal? That is the tightrope Cirque du Soleil must walk if it is to keep its driving design alive and create success built to last.

Design, as we've been discussing it, is a living, ongoing process that has to learn from mistakes, refresh itself, and take new risks all the time. You must keep coming back to the idea of an experience and design toward it, embrace the vigilance of maintaining it, and remember the many facets. That holds true for a product, a service, an entertainment, or even something such as fixed-location retailing. Especially in that environment, the location where you sell your goods demands artful design for the total customer experience.

Design is a living, ongoing process that has to learn from mistakes, refresh itself, and take new risks all the time.

For example, when you go into a Whole Foods Market, you are treated to a designed experience. You don't have to ask where the baskets and carts are. A beam of light from track lighting is directed toward each, catching your eye as you enter. The main entrance

The idea behind Whole Foods is more than being a market. It is an informative, rewarding experience.

is typically through the produce section, where every bin is full, with vegetables and fruits arranged in symmetric rows — shiny, taut, green next to yellow beside red — and a "foodie" clerk is always handy to remove any flawed or fallen produce, or to help with a selection. That informed person is able to tell you the difference between two kinds of onions or which type of ginger you might try. If you have a special need, such as new red potatoes all smaller than a golf ball for a special dish to go with your salmon, a clerk will gladly go into the back and dig through boxes to get you exactly what you need. And when you later go to the fish department to get your salmon fillets, the person behind the counter is likely to throw in a couple lemons "because you'll need these."

Free sample stations stand in most departments so you can have a wedge of apple or a taste of the five-seed farmer's bread. As you pass the cheese section, you "smell" cheese. A large wheel has been cut and placed where the breeze wafts it to you. By the barrels of coffee beans, several pots are brewing and the aroma lures you closer for a sample of today's Kona blend. Throughout the store, you're likely to find places attended to by live people where you can sit at a counter and have a seafood meal, a snack, Italian food, or sushi, each with buckets of different wines coordinated with the meals so you can have a glass in a relaxing moment — an experience.

You can find the row of foods prepared for the busy worker who is stopping by on the way home but wants to prepare a special meal. If you decide to eat at the store, there's also a wide selection of cold and warm foods ready to eat at the tables inside or, better yet, at those outside on the flagstone patio, where a rill of water courses in a small stream between the umbrella-covered tables. As you check out, the wall behind the registers is covered with evidence of the store's involvement in the environment and local community activities. Sure, the prices are, in general, a bit higher than those at the nearest supermarket, but if you don't leave with a warm and fuzzy feeling that you deserve to shop this way, then you haven't been paying attention.

Constant vigilance, we have said, is part of an active, integrated design. Consider a store such as The Sharper Image, where some could argue that the originally innovative design has faded. The original idea was that you would discover all these products and learn from the editorial thread. Part of going to the store was about this experience, similar to browsing a multidimensional magazine. Perhaps you didn't always buy something—you just went there to play with the products. It was really the sort of venue where you could learn about technology with its myriad embodiments, and experience fun and inspirational things. But the stores have too much stuff now and have lost a lot of that editorial thread. They have just filed for chapter 11 bankruptcy protection.

A company that does not interact face-to-face with its customers has a harder time feeling the emotional experience of its customers. Consider Dell, for example. People don't really experience the brand until they get their product. Their contact is only through the Dell web site. The problem is how to interact with and feel what the brand means to customers. It can mean efficiency, currency, and low cost. But does Dell get an answer to the question, "What do the products feel like to the customer?" It's not so easy, rather something to work toward. For a while, Dell put kiosks in malls with people in blue polo shirts to show the products, but the consumers couldn't buy them there, and that led to more confusion than understanding.

Design-driven companies focus on people throughout the process. That's what drives development. It all comes from the idea of creating an emotional response.

When Amazon.com first started, it had to take a number of innovative steps to connect at the emotional level of a customer's experience. How do you have a customer feel more cared for by a web site than when dealing with a live person? (Actually, that's not so hard if you reflect on your average experience at a big-box store.) Making purchases easy and secure was one step. "1 Click" was a stroke of brilliance. Providing a forum to review offerings opened an interactive avenue and created a sense of community that mitigated the fear of buying without touching and feeling. A data system tapped the interests of customers. Whether you were buying for yourself, your children, or your grandparents, you got relationship sales suggestions that often resulted in additional sales for Amazon and a better experience for you. See if most human clerks you talk to remember your personal preferences. But is Amazon bulletproof? No, nothing is. Would you miss it if it went away? We would. Would you?

That leads us to the context of all people in any business. Why is it so important that design be part of all aspects of your business, from one end to the other? What is a design-driven company? It's where any company begins by putting the experience in the center and then working outward from there. You can look at companies whose core offering might be technology or maybe a service, and it's design driven when it's shaped and driven by what customers see, experience, and value. For these companies, that's what drives development—marketing and sales, even manufacturing and distribution. It all comes from the idea of "What are we designing for people, for what emotional response, and how do we do that?"

With the earlier Whole Foods example, we touched on the fact that sometimes people are willing to pay a little more for an experience that is emotionally positive. In that way, design represents part of the value of the equation people will pay a premium for. You are designing for the category of customer you want, the kind willing to pay a premium for a superior experience, as is the case with Whole Foods. In the case of Southwest Airlines, you usually get a better experience for less—how good is that?

So when you're talking about the direction of your company, you have to understand that when people will pay you a premium for an experience that you have designed for them and that they have connected with and value, it's the only thing your competitor can't replicate instantly. United cannot replicate Southwest. When your customers have decided that you matter, it's yours to lose after that. When you do it well and you stay on top of it, it's an unbelievable asset, and you can earn a lot of revenue from it. It's the gift that keeps on giving. However, that doesn't mean you rest on your laurels.

Now, all this is not just a good idea—it's do or die. If your company doesn't embrace the concept of design we've been talking about, the kind that embodies a positive and emotional customer experience, then it could be on life support sometime soon. Many reasons exist why doing business has become so much more challenging. As time goes on, customers become more demanding in terms of design. All you have to do is go to any number of blogs, review sites, or even sales platforms to see candid feedback that motivates companies to improve designs if they want to stay in business. Products and services get better. At least the very best get amazingly good, and the poor, well, the poor get poorer.

Especially here in the United States, during the last ten years of significant growth, a public understanding of design has emerged. People have become more interested in and discerning about how things are, how they work, how they look, and how they behave. This starts to move companies to invest in design. More companies are spending money and time on design—although many of them are still not doing it well. The trend continues to grow.

A broader idea playing out here is that designing a unique and highly valued set of customer experiences is really one of the only truly defensible strategies. If you have your own brand-driven approach to design, others can't really take this from you. People can try to copy it, but then they become merely derivative. If you do a good job at it, you have something that becomes a very strong and defensible strategy. With brilliant customer experience supply chain

If a high level of attention to detail is not designed in, then you're going to be commoditized, and there is no way you are going to win a war of commoditization. You will lose that call.

management, when a customer purchases your product or pays for your service, they feel they have joined something. This goes way beyond just the physicality of the product. It's the totality of the experience of the community of customers, all the people who do business with you, and everyone who uses the products and services you produce and deliver.

Diners at Alice Waters's legendary Chez Panisse *feel* connected to the community of growers and to the very earth itself as they experience memorable delights of wonderful food, naturally and exquisitely prepared from extraordinary ingredients. Waters might not think of herself as an architect of a design-driven business, but we have known her for 30 years and she is also this.

So, if this level of attention to the details of the experience is not designed in, then you're going to be commoditized, and there's no way in the world you can win a war of commoditization. You'll lose that call.

In many ways, Dell is a living example of this reality. Michael Dell is seriously smart. Dell is obviously an extremely successful company built around a brilliantly designed operational model. But because, as a company, it has never completely embraced design with the full spectrum of its customers' total experience at the center, it becomes prey in a commoditized world. For one thing, people have copied Dell's operational model because they can; you can figure it out and do it. As a result, the company now has diluted equity with the consumer. It recently released some terrifically well-designed products and has consistently delivered durable and excellent technology. However, this is not the same as being a design-driven company, and we assert that its market cap suffers in consequence.

Equity with your customer is built over time. It's similar to equity in anything. It builds up, it's stable, and it's there. If you don't build equity, people don't really know who you are.

You build equity over time. When you do it successfully, it's similar to equity in anything: It builds up, it's stable, and it's there. When you don't build equity, people don't really know who you are. When your company is consistent and focused on design and the impact of design on experience, you build up a capital reserve in people's hearts and minds about who you are and that you matter to them. This is a very valuable asset.

The fact is, many companies have consciously gone about creating equity with the customer as part of their strategic plan instead of viewing it as something that happens accidentally along the way. But they don't always include all the elements that really do matter. Dell has built a lot of its equity around pricing, its delivery model, its ability to configure and customize, and its aim to be a business partner. This is all good. But wait — there has to be more. These good things are not sufficiently aspirational or inspirational to bond customers to a company, brand, or product. Dell is working on the "but wait — there has to be more" part. The company has smart people. If Dell believes design of the total customer experience is important (and it is), the company will figure it out.

Some companies, such as Apple, Nike, and BMW, do this consistently well over a long period of time. A surprising consequence is that when a company establishes this enduring commitment to a design-driven culture, focused on the customer experience as the defining criteria of great design, then the customer, in turn, often grants the company the option to fail once in a while. If you're a BMW driver and BMW puts out a less-than-perfect model (and they've had a few that have been stinkers design wise), you cut the company some slack. "This is BMW," you say. "They're just messing around. They're trying something out, and they'll get back on track." On the other hand, if Chevrolet comes out with a clunker, you will probably say, "There you go again, that's Chevrolet for you." Chevrolet has just lived up to your worst expectations, so you have a different response.

When a company establishes this enduring commitment to a design-driven culture, then the customer, in turn, often grants the company the option to fail once in a while.

When a company establishes an idea, people will grasp it and grow it, for better or for worse. It's up to you to create and hold positive equity. It's vital that you do. Depending on the emotional nature of the equity you build, it can leverage you forward or take you down. As a customer, this object or service that you're interacting with is sending you information. When you see it, touch it, and use it, it's giving you information.

This is a really important notion that helps provide the answer to the questions: "Why? Why design or die, and why now?" As Marty Neumeier put it, "We've moved from an economy of mass production to one of mass customization."[4] Products previously were produced in mass quantities, and you had relatively few choices. The amount of capital and time it took to develop a product was so significant that the variables or different options available were generally quite limited. In the last ten (and especially last five) years, the ability to manufacture quickly has grown exponentially along with the ability to manufacture different variations. The ability to configure to order is rapidly growing also.

Consequently, you can no longer make product decisions based on only features and benefits because everybody either has the features and benefits or can get to them fairly quickly. So, as a consumer, on what basis do you now make choices? You make choices on an emotional basis. You make choices based on what the product is saying to you, your connection to a brand you trust, and the qualities and meaning you have invested in that brand.

This describes the current state. But many companies don't fully recognize the importance of the emotional component because this component is not spreadsheet friendly. Rational features and benefit analysis aren't as effective anymore because too much exists for mere mortals. Go buy a TV. How the heck do you start if you're not looking at how it looks, how the picture connects to you, and how the sound quality resonates for you?

If you try to do it by reading resolution specs (let's see, is 1080i good enough, or do I need 1080p?), analyzing features, comparing size, and even comparing price—forget it. How do you make a decision? You will look at them and say, "Well, I know Sony's a good brand, and I know Samsung's a good brand." Then "Oh, I like the way that one looks. It will fit well in my home." And when you see it, "Oh, that picture really jumps out at me, and the sound is great." Those are the things that matter in how people make choices today. That's the crux of why the design experience driving brand connection has become so important. It has always been important but now it's crucial.

If you're not already integrating the design of the customer experience supply chain throughout your company, you need to get cracking. In the next chapter, we take a deeper look at design-driven companies and consider how yours could take steps toward becoming one.

Being Design Driven

Design as a total concept—how iconic design-driven companies behave—a look at what your company needs to do to be design driven—how companies such as Apple, Samsung, and Interactive behave and how design is embedded in their culture.

Let's say you know your company isn't yet the icon you want it to be. Perhaps you've taken a few steps, tentative or assertive, but you aren't yet a design-driven company from one end to the other. Well, you need to be. It isn't easy; otherwise, more companies would be doing it. If your company, products, or services do not live in the gut of your customers as a positive emotional experience, you need to take a candid look at yourself and consider what you need to do to get started and keep going.

This chapter, and those that follow, provide a more "how-to" look at becoming design driven as a company. On your path, you need to progress through the following steps:

- *Awareness* of where you are and where you need to be.

- *Commitment* to taking the leap of faith.

- *Implementation* of some new approaches and people, taking half-steps to full steps.

- *Vigilance* to stay fresh and tap the most current customer needs for emotional experience. You also need to stay on top of every aspect of the customer experience supply chain so that all things that effect design are done properly and are coordinated.

Vigilance is important because companies that previously "got it" have shown that it is possible to "lose it." Rejuvenating and keeping the process alive is up to you. Before you start, you need that first step of awareness. The purpose of this chapter is to explore these topics—to begin to answer the question, "What is a design-driven company?"

Conrad Hilton was famous for a couple things, the least of which is having Paris Hilton as a descendant. He is notably more famous for saying that every member of his hotel staff is on the sales team, from bellhop to mail room clerk, to reservation maker to accountant. Hilton wanted the customer experience to establish a positive emotional connection to his brand. Every detail went toward that. Hilton's hotels were among the first to put an *H* imprint in the white sand of the hallway ashtrays and to fold the toilet tissue into a triangle at the end.[5] The effect was to communicate to the customer, "We're paying attention to every detail of your stay."

Hilton clearly had the customer experience in mind, but did that make his company a design-driven one? No. It wasn't long before competitors were putting an *S* imprint in the sand of their hallway ashtrays, and it wasn't too hard to fold the end of toilet tissue. Competitors on a misguided path even went to extremes of origami, enough to scare away the patrons from some complimentary items in fear of getting a paper cut.

A step toward awareness is recognizing what part of your design a competitor can easily replicate and what amounts to a truly iconic experience that cannot easily be copied.

A design-driven company has commitment from the top. Hilton had it while Conrad was around, but it has since devolved to become just another "respectable" chain. Hilton couldn't retain its iconic quality without focus, vigilance, and freshness. As noted, Apple began to drift during the interlude when Steve Jobs was not present, but it quickly restored focus when he returned. By way of contrast, becoming design driven has proven to be difficult for Dell, which brilliantly built a business using superb traditional supply chain management rather than a focus on an intended customer experience. Companies must champion the commitment to become design driven with a relentless vigilance of the customer experience supply chain. This must start at the top and cascade to every aspect of the way a company operates.

That's why a company doesn't become a design-driven company without continuing executive leadership. It's inevitably difficult, it's not everyone's initial passion, and you might need to do things that you're not comfortable with or that you haven't done before. People

It is important to be aware of what part of what you do is truly iconic and cannot be easily replicated by competitors.

don't perform that way unless they are inspired
to, are forced to, or are given an incentive to do
so—that's human nature. Consequently you need
a champion who understands all this and is willing and able to drive change through the system.

*If you look inside
any design-driven
company, you
will find someone
doing the job of
"chief experience
officer."*

Apple continues to be an excellent example.
Selling 25 million iPods can do that, as can being
named the world's most innovative company multiple times. Yes, we know—you read the press,
and sometimes we all get sick of hearing from
pundits. But the thing of it is, there are too few
examples of companies that have really achieved
this level of mastery when it comes to being
design driven. However, consider this the good
news, because this is also a notice of opportunity
for you to get out there and lead a parade. If you
look inside any design-driven company, you will
find someone doing the job of chief experience
officer. It's what to do if you're not Steve Jobs
because you don't have to be the chief executive
officer to be the chief experience officer. It just
so happens that Jobs holds both jobs (couldn't
resist that one), but it doesn't have to be this way.

Back to Apple. What is it really about on
the inside? What it's about, according to Apple's
Senior Vice President of Design, Jonathan Ive,
who was the 2003 winner of London's Design
Museum inaugural Designer of the Year award,
"Not only is it critical that the leadership of a
company clearly understands its products and
the role of design, but that the development,
marketing, and sales teams are also equally
committed to the same goals. More than ever,
I am aware that what we have achieved with
design is massively reliant on the commitment
of lots of different teams to solve the same
problems and on their sharing the same goals."[6]

Ive says this is the reason so many new products are bland and derivative: "So many companies are competing against each other with similar agendas. Being superficially different is the goal of so many of the products we see. A preoccupation with differentiation is the concern of many corporations rather than trying to innovate and genuinely taking the time, investing the resources, and caring enough to try and make something better."

Consider these characteristics of Apple's design-driven experience:

- **Driven from the top**—The senior team is thoroughly committed to not only championing the design-driven strategy, but also making design and innovation a feature of the company's DNA. According to Ive, this is a major part of Apple's success as a design-driven company.

- **Design-driven focus**—Design is not applied as an afterthought or window dressing; it is a starting point. Design isn't primarily about good looks, either. It's about solving a problem by blending function and usability, often in an iconic style, to create an emotional connection with the intended customer. As Jobs tells it, it is about making products "that people love."

- **Thinking differently**—Greatness is not achieved by doing like everybody else. By thinking differently, you can make a difference. In some ways, Apple's iPod had fewer features than competitors' products, but the design of the feature set functioned

> *"A preoccupation with differentiation is the concern of many corporations rather than trying to innovate."*
> *— Jonathan Ive*

to provide a better customer experience. People do get to love their iPods.

- **Quick to prototype and market**—A design-driven company doesn't labor on a product until it's perfect. To quote Jobs, "Artists ship." Instead, a design-driven company launches new products quickly and often, and it improves on them in response to consumer feedback. Recall how the iPod came out with a Windows-friendly version during its first year of release.

When you look at the companies that excel at design and are driven by it, you can see that they are, from the very beginning, searching for the right opportunity; they're already thinking about the experience design possibility. When they find the opportunity, they begin to design it. When they move into engineering, the design of both the physical and emotional elements is very important to engineer. The emotional elements are not something to be eliminated because of costs. You have to figure out how to do it. Same thing in manufacturing. The selection of quality materials and how parts go together (fit and finish) must be an integral part of the design. Companies can't view it as "Oh, we're spending an extra 50¢—let's cut that out." You must figure out how to do it, and then get the product into distribution.

Design-driven companies manufacture to the way they design instead of designing to the way they manufacture.

Consider another instructional and compelling Apple example: When the company creates something, it doesn't force it into an existing manufacturing line and then wait to see what happens. When the product design uses clear plastic, the company actually changes all the lighting in the manufacturing facility, and everyone wears gloves. The company builds its line around the reality that "we have to maintain the quality of these parts": People need to be able to see the parts as the product moves along through a scratch-free system. Apple spends the money to do that. Another company might just say, "Let's throw it on this line," and then "Oh, we're having a lot of defects. This is too expensive—we can't be doing this. The reject rate is too high." Design must carry into every corner of the process and, of course, into the promotion and into the market. That's the idea of being design driven. It's a process, not an event. It's just the way you do things.

Design-driven companies manufacture to the way they design instead of designing to the way they manufacture.

It's important to understand how you become design driven. You don't just flip a switch and make it an overnight event. You need to give it time. Progress is usually non-linear.

Apple did not start out as design-driven as it has become. As Apple focused on customer experience (above a lot of distractions), it became so. During the Scully years, the pioneering Apple Industrial Design Group was established by Brunner. It continued to do great design and build an exceptionally talented design team. But at the same time, management grew to misunderstand what Apple was really good at and what really mattered. Focus was quickly restored when Jobs returned and saw how the business had drifted. He realized that the company was not leveraging the full capabilities of a unique design infrastructure.

Design, as we discuss it here, is really a methodology you use to shape and create the relationship between you and your customer. Design means you are overtly creating, developing, prototyping, and manufacturing with customer emotion in mind, not just letting all this evolve and happen. Most companies go about doing their business in their little silos. Working independently, they concoct an experience in a haphazard way. Then they try to shape it all—this isn't working here, let's fix this one, then we'll jump to this one. Although they might incrementally improve things, they aren't aligned in any sort of "where are we going?" way.

Executing great design is everybody's job, not just the designer's.

Design is everybody's business. And if a CEO is going to do it right, he or she needs to understand this. As you think about becoming a more design-driven company, you can use baby steps and big steps. But if you want to know in a nutshell, what do you need to do; you must build a development process that centers on people and an experience. You must give everyone an incentive to be an active part of this process. You must build a marketing process that can characterize and communicate those design ideas to people emphasizing design as an integral part of it all. You need to build an engineering system that understands that the people driving design sensibility and values are, at the same time, part of the marketing, engineering, manufacturing, and delivery equations.

So if you want to become more design savvy, you need to understand that it's a total concept. You can't just jam an in-house design department into place, like some airplane passenger who's stuck between the two fat people in row 26. You'll have to manage relationships among all the constituents and the stakeholders in the process. In product design, a classic dog vs. cat battle usually emerges between the industrial designer and the engineer. The engineer is always saying, "I'm not the artsy guy, and what's all this stuff about how or what people should feel?" The industrial designer is saying to the engineer, "I don't care if you have to walk over flaming coals to do it—just do it." Then all of engineering rolls its collective eyeballs to the chorus, "Here go the stylists again. They don't know about engineering or manufacturing, and they're screwing up this company."

One of the most critical aspects of creating a good product is the relationship between the designer and the engineer—it's not a natural or easy one. You have to ensure shared values, a shared understanding, and a shared commitment—all reinforced by the right incentives and rewards that matter to each individual.

If you're a designer, you can make one object perfectly. It's a much greater challenge to make thousands, tens of thousands, hundreds of thousands, or millions. You can't do that without the support of very talented engineering and manufacturing teams. You have to build that relationship and ensure that people understand why it's valuable to spend the extra time and money. Then you need to respect the technical expertise that you work with and help them build the product. You also need to monitor the relationship with manufacturing and then how the product is delivered to the consumer. You can learn a lot when you watch a customer unpack your product. Are they delighted or not? Did you make a good first impression? You need to know. We're talking about managing the entire customer experience supply chain.

In summary, a sequence of events drives a design-driven company:

- The customer need

- The product that emotionally answers that need

- The orchestration of design, manufacturing, and delivery of that product to the customer

- The vigilance to keep looking ahead to the next customer need and the next product

That's the cycle, and the process need not be painful once everyone understands the deal and has the right incentive. Then you roll forward to continuing profitability. With that in mind, let's take a look at a company or two where this works well—and a couple where it turned out their cornbread wasn't baked all the way through to the middle.

Positive Examples of Design-Driven Companies

Sticking with some big names for a moment, we have BMW, IKEA, Nike, and Samsung. The IKEA business concept is a terrific case in point. Its catalogue and user manual enable customers to do their own interior design and assemble the furniture—all part of its value to the customer. Instead of just being a consumer, the customer becomes a coproducer or cocreator, filled with an experience of achievement.

Samsung is currently rated as the number-one brand in consumer electronics, yet as recently as 15 years ago, it was regarded as a second-tier manufacturer of cheap elec- tronics. What happened?

Now let's look to a big-name company that, while it may not be exactly like your own, made a dynamic shift from business as usual to become a design-driven company. We speak here of Samsung, where there are lessons for us all.

Design for the Seoul–Samsung's Turnaround

In 2006, *BusinessWeek* rated Samsung as 20th on the top 100 global brands list and number 1 in the electronics industry. *Business Week* also placed Samsung as number 12 in a ranking of the "Top 100 Most Innovative Companies" in a special report published on April 24, 2006. In January 2007, *BrandFinance* ranked the company as the number-one global brand in electronics.

Yet as recently as 15 years ago, some regarded Samsung as just a second-tier manufacturer of cheap electronics. What happened?

In 1994, Samsung's chairman, Kun-Hee Lee, who had a net worth in the billions and was one of the richest and arguably the most power-ful man in South Korea, began transforming the company into a design-driven one when he aimed to sell top-quality branded electronics products at premium prices. To accomplish this, the company needed the cultural equivalent of an extreme makeover to envision products that would appeal to the much broader global mar-ket. The company already had a design staff and frequently hired design consultants. However, the results had been inconsistent. So Lee, who had spent his college years in Japan and the United States, hired a Japanese design consul-tant to take a hard and honest look at Samsung's strengths and weaknesses. The verdict was a surprise. The consultant said Samsung already had world-class designers on its staff; the prob-lem was in the process.

Lee sent 17 Samsung employees to the Art Center College in Pasadena to see what they could learn about creating a similar design facil-ity in Seoul. In return, the school sent a team of its people to Seoul, where Gordon Bruce, an industrial design consultant who acted as the school's liaison with Japan, and James Miho, chairman of the school's Graphic, Packaging, and Electronic Media Department, were among those invited to Lee's house for dinner. This was a rare treat because Lee is a virtual recluse who rarely visits his own company sites. Lee had in mind an Innovation Design Lab, eventually known as *ids*, which was to be housed in an eight-story $10 million building in Seoul. He asked Bruce to serve as chairman of product design and Miho as chairman of new media.

The design-driven path they laid out had to weave its way through as many downs as ups, but the futuristic innovating spirit of looking to consumer electronics needs generated an array of high-definition TVs, computer monitors, digital cell phones, video cameras, music players, and still cameras. Meanwhile, Sony, once the company everyone looked to for electronic products, had channeled much of its money into the music and movie industries. Its U.S. executives had become so paranoid about piracy that they were reticent about approving product capabilities that could possibly be used for duplicating digital media files. Samsung surged into the vacuum, but not without that occasional dip in the road that comes with taking risks.

In a *Wired* article,[7] Frank Rose describes a rare visit by Lee to one of Samsung's biggest plants in Gumi, a south-central Korean factory town. Lee had sent out Samsung's new wireless phones as a 1995 New Year's gift, only to learn they didn't work. Something was about to hit the fan, and no one would be confusing the fragrance with Chanel Number 5. As Rose put it, "At Lee's command, the factory's 2,000 employees donned headbands labeled 'Quality First' and assembled in a courtyard. There they found their entire inventory piled in a heap—cell phones, fax machines, nearly $50 million worth of equipment. A banner before them read 'Quality Is My Pride.' Beneath the banner sat Lee and his board of directors. Ten workers took the products one

At Samsung, engineers had previously defined new products and decided what features to give them; now specialists in everything from industrial design to the cognitive sciences would embrace that role.

by one, smashed them with hammers, and threw them into a bonfire. Before it was over, employees were weeping."

In his New Year's address, Lee proclaimed 1996 as the Year of Design Revolution, referring to design in the broadest sense—not just styling, but consumer research and marketing as well. Engineers had previously defined new products and decided what features to give them; now specialists in everything from industrial design to the cognitive sciences would embrace that role. "Most of us didn't understand what he was talking about," says Kook-Hyun Chung, the senior vice president who heads the Corporate Design Center in Seoul. "Now we understand that we have a new, bigger, broader responsibility."

But another dip in the road loomed ahead. Part of Samsung's strength was its vertically integrated, globally networked manufacturing, which enabled it to save millions by making its own memory chips and LCD screens. By 1997, the market for memory chips plunged. At the same time, the Korean currency, the won, plummeted (along with all the overextended East Asian currencies) to half its value, pushing Samsung toward bankruptcy. In response, Samsung had to eliminate businesses and lay off as many as 24,000 factory employees—30 percent of its workforce—and move much of its manufacturing to other locations in Mexico, Brazil, Hungary, Slovakia, China, and Malaysia. In 2000, the company took another hit when it tried to enter the automobile business.

How a design-driven company handles its setbacks, as well as successes, shows through. By staying tuned to design and using consumer research as a window to emerging needs and possibilities, Samsung was quick to make the shift from analog to digital. As the Korean economy recovered, the company outstripped many of its competitors with products such as a 56-inch DLP high-definition television—a U.S. Super Bowl party animal's dream. What made it all work? A driving eye to the global consumer market of the future, not the past. As Rose describes it, "Samsung put together an elite creating new businesses (CNB) group to explore long-term social and technological trends that could spark new product lines."

CNB is one of Samsung's secret weapons: a team of designers from different business units who look into the future. Ki-seol Koo, the vice president who heads the organization, was a TV designer who found his new assignment bewildering at first. "There was no agenda," he recalls. "We were just told to come up with something. Normally you have a road map to follow—you know what's going to happen months from now. But this was blank." Now the unit's approximately 30 members develop animated what-if films and 3D mock-ups to show top executives how products might be used in some future world. "It's not about what's happening now," Koo says. "It's about imagining what our living environment will be like five or ten years down the road."[8]

Interface Gets in the Face of Business as Usual

Going "green" is all the rage these days, but one of the first companies to see this light, respond to it, and actually benefit at the bottom line was a company called Interface. With annual net sales of more than a billion dollars, Interface is the world's largest manufacturer of commercialized floor coverings.

If you've ever needed carpet hauled to a landfill, you know it comes with a whopping fee because of the nonbiodegradable content of carpets. Interface was generating tons of solid, liquid, and gaseous waste during production, not to mention more than 920 million square yards of used carpet being heaved into U.S. landfills annually. Ray C. Anderson, CEO, had an enlightening experience in 1994 when he read *The Ecology of Commerce* (Collins, 1994), by Paul Hawken. He was not merely moved; he decided to do something about it, and that something involved design.

Changing the business from one that hadn't given a second thought to its impact on the environment for more than 20 years to one making a conscious effort to clean up its act meant reinventing the carpet-making business to become environmentally friendly, and becoming aware of how to make positive changes to its product at every stage of its life cycle.

The company's design consultant, David Oakey, was reluctant to buy into the new vision. When he gathered a group of people from all over the company to investigate the notion, they came to some surprising conclusions. Chief among these was that the company had been designing its products poorly in the first place. The group members considered ways to eliminate waste when making the products, such as using less fiber. They considered what materials could be recycled and ended up eliminating

waste in the manufacturing process. They also put an end product that could be recycled at the front end of their considerations. And that, along with the other steps, serendipitously helped lead to two of the company's most innovative brands.

With one of the products, named Wabi, Oakey asked his manufacturing people if they could make the pile lower. When he kept insisting that it be lower than what they came up with, one technician, in an outburst of frustration, suggested that if he wanted the pile that low, why didn't he just turn the carpet upside down? That actually worked. Customers loved the simple, minimal look that fit the growing trend toward hard finishes and away from textiles. Serendipity can be a real part of how a design-driven culture strikes gold.

At Interface, the goal was to manufacture in a sustainable way. That goal has forced the company to be more creative in rethinking everything it does, and it has led to doing things in better ways with lower costs.

Something similar happened with Solenium, another breakaway success for Interface. In a discussion about the success of Wabi, someone said that it was a shame the company couldn't make carpet out of recycled pop bottles the way it did with Teratex, one of its paneling fabrics. That led to the invigorating question of "Why not?" The result was Solenium, a carpet with the look and feel of fabric, the cleanability of vinyl, and the serviceability of replaceable squares. A lot of educational and health care facilities found it perfect for their needs.

As it turned out, the path to thinking differently about every consumer need, was also the creative path to carpet tiles that can fit any sized space and eliminated many carpet sample books in favor of better-illustrated catalogs and Internet samples (www.thesamplecenter.com). Making 100-percent recycled and recyclable products is one step, but the goal was to manufacture in a sustainable way. That goal has forced the company to be more creative in rethinking everything it does, and it has led to doing things in better ways with lower costs. The green that Interface was aiming for also turned out to be the color of money.

Getting on Target with Target

Yogi Berra once said, "When you come to a fork in the road, take it." That's exactly what the mass-merchandise chain Target did. Founded in 1962, about the same time Kmart and Wal-Mart began, it has defined itself by taking a different direction. Although Kmart and Wal-Mart are both price oriented, Target has consciously aimed to be design oriented. It might generate only $60 billion a year, compared to Wal-Mart's $350 billion a year. And Target might have only 352,000 employees, compared to Wal-Mart's almost two million employees as the nation's largest employer (a good chunk of whom must be just generating W-2 forms). But Target is quite comfortable with its particular niche. A Gallup poll on mass-merchandising trends in 2002[9] indicated that only 16 percent of shoppers polled with incomes of $20,000 or less choose Target, but that climbs to 47 percent among those with annual earnings of $75,000 or more. The median age of Target shoppers is 37, and 80 percent have attended college;[10] 97 percent of American consumers recognize the Target bull's-eye logo.

Target has targeted the yuppie and puppy yuppie shoppers with designs that are fun, unpredictable, yet still affordable. It attracts these customers with unique products designed

Target has attracted a desirable segment of shoppers by featuring unique products designed by well-known designers such as Michael Graves.

by the likes of Michael Graves, Isaac Mizrahi, Mossimo Giannulli, Fiorucci, Liz Lange, and Philippe Starck. Graves's work, for instance, tickles the emotional fancy with chubby toasters, whimsical teakettles, sleek candleholders, and egg-shaped utensils. The egg shape is part of his signature style, and it has begun to appear on Target's garden furniture and timepieces as well. The scale of producing these goods for nearly a thousand stores enables the store's customer base to enjoy such eclectic goods.

The products are only part of the design. Target also distinguishes itself with other store-wide touches that contribute to the jokingly French pronunciation of "Tar-zhay" that many customers use. These differentiators are all part of Target's overall design:

- No Muzak or ambient music

- No promotions through a public address system

- Wider aisles

- Drop ceilings

- Artful displays of merchandise

- Cleaner fixtures

- References to customers as "guests"

- No firearms or even realistic firearm toys sold

- No tobacco products sold

So Target might be fifth in size behind Wal-Mart, The Home Depot, Kroger, and Costco, but it remains first in the hearts of many of its selective customers, and it achieves this by design.

Some Not So Positive Examples

A point we'd like to emphasize is that even companies that get on the path of being design driven might have rogue cells in their DNA that can multiply into a potentially fatal flaw. The risk is almost always to do with losing that magic that got them where they were and backing away from a living approach that ensured freshness and ongoing vision. They might have developed success-induced megalomania, slipped into rigid thinking, not understood how they got there in the first place, or not fully committed to being design driven.

Starbucks Slips in Coffee

Just a few short years ago, it seemed everyone was singing the praise of Starbucks, a company that seemed destined to have one of its shops on every street corner of every city. At first, the success story was all about the customer experience. Then suddenly, news came of Starbucks pulling back on its expansion plans. What happened? After growing to nearly 15,000 stores, the first quarter of 2008 marked a 3 percent decrease in U.S. transactions. Shouldn't that number have gone up?

Let's face it—at $4 for a cup of coffee, you're not just buying a cup of coffee. You're paying for a unique experience, a trip to Milan to sit at a sidewalk café. You're paying for a carefully selected bean that is handled and brewed in the best way. The air is alive with the smell of

At $4 for a cup of coffee, you're not just buying a cup of coffee. You're paying for an experience. But here you see the making of the flaw. With a Starbucks wherever you go, the experience is hardly unique anymore.

freshly brewing coffee. You're in a clean, well-lighted place, as Hemingway would put it. It's a social place where you can meet others. And you're getting something you can't get just anywhere.

Here you see the making of the flaw. With a Starbucks wherever you go, the experience is hardly unique anymore. Furthermore, the experience is subject to commoditization. Witness the McDonald's chain addition of coffee baristas to many of its stores. And now you can get Café Select at 7-Eleven convenience stores. Starbucks is even available in vending machines. The hip drink of the 1990s threatens to become the ho-hum drink of the new millennium, and the sales numbers are the slip that's showing. Did we also mention that Starbucks' market cap walked off a cliff?

What happened to the ambience and style that led Starbucks' director of creative services to be referred to as "the keeper of the look"? Myra Gose, who filled that role until 1997 when she left after spending 18 months planning for the chain's birthday party, once said, "All our design, whether it's a packaged food or a new mug, needs to make sense and tell what we're about." So what happened?

For one, the magnificent La Marzocco traditional espresso machines were replaced with soulless super-automatics. They're easy to use for the recently hired "barista" (even Homer Simpson on a bad day could use one), but it's a far step from that trip to Milan. In the face of increasing competition and a diluted uniqueness of experience, it was hardly the time to be cutting corners. The experience was further diminished by a number of other merchandising ploys (deals with music companies, sandwiches, and so on) that all defused the original focus of providing a unique experience.

What's the company to do? Perhaps taking a cue from Apple, in January 2007, the company brought back Howard Schultz, who founded today's Starbucks in 1987.[11] He openly stated his intention to "reignite the emotional attachment between the consumer and the coffee."[12] With stock selling at that time for about half of what it sold for the previous year, Schulz planned some drastic measures. He placed approximately 100 underperforming stores on the block, and he phased out the warmed breakfast sandwiches because "the scent of the warmed sandwiches interferes with the coffee aromas in our stores." Starbucks began to market-test an 8-ounce short cup of coffee priced at $1 (let's see, a Starbucks for a buck—there's a concept).

The company also announced 600 layoffs, and the temporary closing of its 7,100 U.S. stores for three hours of employee training. The coffee chain said the in-store training program would foster enthusiasm in its 135,000 U.S. employees and improve the quality of drinks made by Starbucks baristas. "We believe that this is a bold demonstration of our commitment to our core and a reaffirmation of our coffee leadership," said chief executive Schultz in a statement.[13] We're not filled with warm fuzzies yet.

Is it too little, too late? That will depend on whether Starbucks is able to reinvent itself. Apple pulled that off when Jobs returned. Starbucks seeks to do the same with the return of Schultz.

Polaroid Loses Focus Lock

Yep, that sound you heard was from Polaroid, a once-proud design-conscious company, as it swirled and let out a gasp as it headed down the porcelain bowl.

The Polaroid story begins with a designer, Edwin Land, who dropped out of Harvard after only one year and invented a polarizing film just in time for it to be used in World War II for photo reconnaissance. From the 1950s through the 1970s, Polaroid made most of its money from its camera that went color in 1972—the legendary SX-70. Ideas kept percolating in the company, including the special cameras used for passports and security badges, Polaroid sunglasses, 3D movie glasses, and the not-so-successful Polavision that was a flop in 1978.

By the 1990s, Polaroid was still trying to be design driven, but it wasn't quite making the connection to what was going on in the world around them. The suddenly ubiquitous one-hour photo labs initially threatened the instant-picture concept; then the arrival of the digital camera drove a spike through its heart. The company was in debt equal to 42 percent of its capital in 1995 when Gary Di Camillo came on board as CEO; five years later, that amount had grown to 60 percent. Marketing and administration took 37 percent of what came in from sales. Polaroid was a listing ship that would soon be sinking.

As Wally Bock put it, "By the end of the 1990s, Polaroid was thrashing around like a drowning swimmer. First they were concentrated on new product innovation. In 1998, they introduced 25 new products. Similar numbers followed in 1999 and 2000. There were lots of

© Polaroid Corporation

Polaroid should have driven one-touch simplicity and immediacy into digital. Instead it squandered billions of dollars of the consumer equity it had created.

products, but many weren't very good and the good ones were late to market."[14] It wasn't until 2000 that Di Camillo decided Polaroid should become a "digital imaging company," long after the competition was firmly entrenched in that market. Polaroid should have driven one-touch simplicity and immediacy into digital. Instead it squandered billions of dollars of the consumer equity it had created.

Again, see the irony here: The company that invented instant photography was beaten into irrelevance by the invention of *digital* instant photography. Polaroid's failure to understand the essence of its customers' experience and the emotional thrill of *instant* was a fatal flaw. It built a technology company on customer delight and failed to notice customers' changing needs and interests. As they say, if you can't be a shining example, you'll just have to be a terrible warning. Consider yourself warned.

Implementation

So you can start with a product, hire a consultant, and reorganize from within, but total commitment from top to bottom must eventually rule the day if you are to become truly design driven. Let's say you hire a consultant to work on one product with you. You let that consultant work with your team and you give the consultant your support. Together you can drive that one product through, although you'll endure some bruises along the way. But if you want to do it over the long term, you need to start looking at the overall structure of things—how resources are allocated, how people are given incentives,

Being design driven is a process, not an event. Unless you are willing to make some fundamental changes, you'll go back to doing things the way you did.

what the culture is, and how you can operate from a customer-experience perspective. Learn what you can change, because that's how you achieve longevity.

That's why being design driven is a process, not an event. *You can do an event once, but unless you make some fundamental changes, you'll go back to doing things the way you did.*

To use Dell as an example, one of the general managers asked us to look at the company's overall product-design experience from the concept to delivery and beyond, and evaluate the flow to see how to improve it all. The inquiry unearthed a tangle. When we looked at all the organizations that impacted what came in the box to the customer, we found that they didn't communicate with each other. They didn't have a shared strategy or vision. Resources were allocated across industrial design, engineering, manufacturing, packaging, and instructional products in a way that was inconsistent with building the kind of design-driven capabilities we have discussed. Nobody had any performance criteria around design. Nobody got a bonus for creating a really great design and designing a great customer experience. They all got a bonus if it was delivered on time, if they reduced cost, or if they met other similar criteria.

We told the manager we could do the strategy piece and could give him a common approach and set of values for everyone to use when creating materials. But to make any significant change, we told him, the company needed to restructure. It needed to reallocate resources and change people's incentives. At the time, the company wasn't willing to do any of this because it was just too difficult. Its approach was more like this: "Okay, we'll pay you some money and you'll write a document—we'll distribute it to everybody, and then it's back to business (as usual)." To really be a design-driven company, you have to be willing to reengineer the way things are done. Yes, once again, Dell has put out some really good-looking products lately. Our wish for the company is for it to become a master of customer experience supply chain management, because their mastery of commodity supply chain management will not sustain them.

When you're starting a design strategy for your company, you can think of it similar to the architecture of a building. In that light, we would say, "The first thing about a brand or a product line is that you've got legacy. And you cannot quickly divorce yourself from a legacy. It's there—you have to recognize it." A lot of companies make a mistake here. They say, "We're known for a bad design experience, so we're changing that tomorrow; we're coming out with a new product." And your customer will look at it and say, "Oh, hey, that's kind of a nice thing from company X, but I still remember all the other crap they put out. They'll never keep this up."

Our recommendation is that you look at this as two tiers. On the lower tier is the legacy. You want to embrace your positive legacy. You want to take the things you're known for—how people feel about you, the good aspects—with you into the future. When Microsoft asked us to take a look at Windows, we came up with these three words: *qualified, understated,* and *reliable.* By *qualified,* we mean that it's a standard. People know it—it's Microsoft. It's an entity that obviously is here and will continue to be here. The product is understated in the sense of productivity and professionalism. And it's reliable—not in the sense that it doesn't crash, but that most people don't worry that Microsoft will disappear tomorrow. Then you ask, "How do I build on top of that? How can we change the idea and the experience to be different?"

How Do You Know How Your Customers Feel?

What you really want to do is get out and understand what people are doing, how they're doing it, what's going on in their lives, what their issues are, and what problems they face. You have to learn what a phrase such as "it just works" means to them. You need to not only see and hear this concept, but also understand it at a level that helps you look for opportunities. You need to step outside your own little box and immerse yourself until you feel that you have made a genuine and usable discovery. Then out of that discovery, you build a map of ideas, opinions, and assumptions, and you go off and create stuff. Later, you need to go back and validate against those assumptions.

From your discovery process, you should learn that this idea of yours is something people need; this is the way they do things now; and this is how they want to do it. You go off and design to that specification. Then you put what you've designed back in front of the people who revealed the need you discovered. You say, "Okay, use it," and you wait and see what happens. You notice that one guy can't find the on-off switch, another person can't get the lid open easily, and another person has trouble reading a screen. You are validating your assumptions, learning whether you've hit them or missed.

If, on the other hand, you start by saying, "OK, we're going to do this product—let's ask people what they like," you wind up with the sort of mediocre outcome that comes of designing by committee. When people think as a group, they end up liking a bland type of product because that's what makes most of them feel comfortable.

If you go develop your product and later play show-and-tell again, the group might say, "Yeah, yeah, I like that." So you bring it to market, and lo and behold, everything out there has changed and moved forward, and what you now have is a boring product that's based on the collective opinions of the 7 out of 12 people who liked it. We refer to it as the "7 out of 12 syndrome." You'll be basing your entire business strategy on the fact that 7 people out of a group of 12 expressed a "like" in a certain direction.

We like to refer to focus group thinking as the "7 out of 12 syndrome," in which you'll be basing your entire business strategy on the fact that 7 people out of a group of 12 expressed a "like" in a certain direction.

At Apple, someone would come in from HP, Sun, or wherever, and really struggle with this concept for a while. They would say "Wait a minute, you guys are putting all this effort into this stuff, but you're not consumer-testing it." They wanted to apply all the usual corporate process-driven metrics. This path can lead to death, or at least mediocrity. Mediocrity is what you end up with if you try to make something everybody likes. Apple didn't target the iPod at everybody. Research and testing can be a deadly double-edged sword. You need to be very clear about what you want to learn and what you can draw from it.

What happens with a lot of companies when they do that kind of research is they put a design in front of customers and say, "What do you think?" And the customers say, "Well, I don't know; I don't know if I like this; it's new; it's scaring me; it's too big; it's too round; it's too square." That's the kind of responses you get. People who use this kind of research come back and say to the designers, "People think this is too square—you've got to make it more round." Most customers have a difficult time articulating their design preferences. You can do far better by watching, listening, and observing.

Cost Factors

A lot of people and companies like to put the cart before the horse and talk about cost first. Well, if cost is everything, you might find yourself sitting beside the road with your hat in your hand while other companies take a risk and surge around you. However, out of respect for these general concerns, let's talk about costs for a moment. Yes, it's true that being design driven is initially more expensive because you'll need to invest time and money doing things you haven't done before that you need to learn to do well. Initially, the product cost might be more because you will run into processes and technical issues that you haven't ironed out or fully considered as you move to the future.

Where a lot of companies fail is they give up the first time because they can't figure it out right away.

The thing about Apple is that they will create something that might initially be more expensive, but the company realizes it's fine for this first time around—they'll figure out how to choreograph the cost out of it. That's the great thing about the human experience—if you place really good people on an idea and give them a clear directive, eventually they figure it out. Where a lot of companies fail is they give up the first time because they can't figure it out right away.

Go ahead and build it the way you want the first time. Give it your best shot, and then set loose your army of operational maniacs to figure out how to eke out the pennies. Along the way, be really grounded on what makes or breaks the design and the experience. If you start with too many constraints— that it has to be a great design, but it can't cost another 10¢ over what it does today, and we have to build it in our existing factory—then you end up only nominally better in the short run and inevitably worse off in the long run.

The Human Factor

Whether you are recruiting for design-driven talent or you want to send your current executives to a school that will immerse them in customer-experience thinking, the good news is that such places exist.

Stanford University's D-School is one such place. Consider its stated mission:

> We believe true innovation happens when strong multidisciplinary groups come together, build a collaborative culture, and explore the intersection of their different points of view. Many talk about multidisciplinary collaboration, but few are actually successful at sustaining attempts to see what will happen. Even

strong partners often lose interest because they cannot get along well enough or long enough to see the fruits of the collaboration. We believe having designers in the mix is key to success in multidisciplinary collaboration and critical to uncovering unexplored areas of innovation. Designers provide a methodology that all parties can embrace and a design environment conducive to innovation. In our experience, design thinking is the glue that holds these kinds of communities together and makes them successful.[15]

Other schools with programs or courses include The Institute of Design (ID) at the Illinois Institute of Technology, Harvard Business School's course "Managing the Innovation Process," Northwestern's "Product Development and Design" class, Georgetown's "Developing New Products and Services" class, an elective at the University of Michigan's Stephen M. Ross School of Business, the Product Development track for MBAs at Carnegie Mellon University's Tepper School of Business, the Haas School of Business at the University of California at Berkeley, the University of Pennsylvania's Wharton School executive program ("Design, Innovation, and Strategy"), and INSEAD's joint program with the Art Center College of Design in Pasadena.

According to a *Business Week* article, "With MBA enrollments down … schools are striving to become more relevant to prospective students."[16] The need for a creative component that understands the customer experience is increasing. *BusinessWeek* says one indication is that "many companies are going directly to top design firms to set up customized executive-education sessions. Most of these involve getting the CEO and his top managers out shopping for the things their company sells. It's a game of 'be your customer' that, despite its simplicity, can have enormous impact. Samsung has learned a great deal about design by attending various sessions at IDEO and other consulting firms."

If you look at most of the Ivy League's business school structure, it delivers captains of industry that should wear a *handicapped* sign with respect to design sensibilities.

The next chapter explores how the design-driven concept needs to extend to your brand and uncovers how your brand is way more than just your company's logo.

5

Your Brand Is Not Your Logo

Why your brand is not what you say it is—How your brand is an experience that lives in your customer's gut—The role of design in brands built to last—How to communicate what your brand is about.

A road-weary family of five climbs out of a Volvo station wagon and heads past the dance hall that won't be open for three more hours toward the post office/saloon that also serves as a souvenir store and is the main business in downtown Luckenbach, a metropolis comprised of four wooden buildings that haven't seen fresh paint in years. Mom, Dad, the twin girls, and their older brother Chip are nearly to the door, anxious to see the place Willie Nelson, Waylon Jennings, Gary P. Nunn, and a host of other country-western singers have all proclaimed as "the" place to go if you are traveling through Texas.

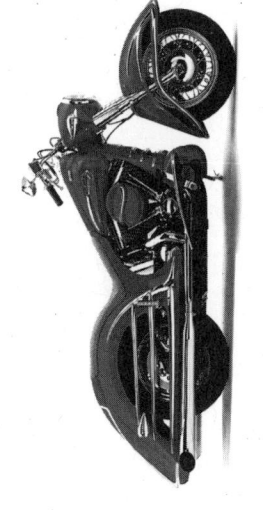

Then they hear the rumble. The deep-throated growl of twenty odd V-Twin engines heading their way. Around the bend they come, two wheels each and glittering in the sun. "Holy, Hunter S. Thompson," Dad yells. "It's the Hell's Angels." Mom clutches the kids close.

From the other direction, half again as many bikers come down from the western turn of the drive. Mom and Dad tremble some, and at least two of the kids eye the nearby outhouse long-ingly. Then something surreal happens.

The bikers pull up, one by one, in a row, their bikes organized and shining. The riders kill the engines, climb off one-by-one, and as each one dismounts, he or she is greeted by others. They hug, kid each other, and compare bikes. The insignia on each bike proclaims it is a Harley-Davidson—the same insignia adorning most jackets, hats, and shirts. Many riders display Harley-Davidson tattoos. It turns out one group is from Tyler, another from Brownsville, while a sprinkling of another group from Waco has mingled in. There is a lot to discuss and share. These riders are not anything close to being a destructive biker gang; they are part of a brotherhood of the road. The family relaxes, aware they are as safe as they would be at a Kiwanis meeting. Their mood shifts to excitement and curiosity, and in that they have something in the bikers. Young Chip feels a tingle in his stomach that might lead him to one day buy a Harley himself.

Few brands have taken on as much of a life of their own as has that of the Harley. Long since the days of movies such as *Wild One* and *Easy Rider*, the Harley has become a revered American icon, standing for the spirit of letting the wind rip through your hair (or across your helmet) on the open road, living free and proud, and feeling the road sweep through every part of you with your senses fully alive. Now, compare that to sitting on the couch with chips and a beverage until the cushions take the shape of your body.

Few could have predicted the bike once known as the Harley "hog," a bad boy's bike, would become the stuff of spontaneous camaraderie for a widely divergent group of individuals who have in common a passion to ride the highways and the backroads of America on two wheels. While there may be sleeker bikes or faster bikes, they all want to do their riding on *this* bike. Picture Malcolm Forbes on the back of his Harley beside Liz Taylor on the one he bought for her. Yes, the Harley has come a long way. But allow yourself no confusion here. The classic Harley-Davidson logo is *not* the company's brand. Instead, the brand is alive in the psyches of all who just rode into town in Luckenbach; it's also alive in those who buy Harley pajamas for their two-year-old; and it's alive in the desire for all those window and bumper stickers, even (especially) the tattoos. The Harley brand is alive in the guts of its customers.

The Harley-Davidson logo is not the company's brand. Instead, the brand is alive in the hearts and psyches of all who ride their machines.

No one knows that more than William G. Davidson, vice president of styling at Harley and grandson of William Davidson, one of the founders. Willie G., as he is known, oversees the design of every Harley model. The classic V-Twin engine is one of the unique aspects he most treasures. But the bike has by no means stayed the same. Every year the company is on the move to incorporate improvements, but without altering the classic look and feel of the bike. A lot of the changes come directly from customer feedback, and the "staying close to the customer" policy comes easy because, as Willie G. puts it, "All the folks at Harley are riders themselves."

Every detail of the Harley stores and merchandise reflects the quality of premium craftsmanship and embodies the lifestyle of the Harley biker. Yes, there might be faster bikes and quieter bikes, but while competition is selling a product, Harley is more than aware it is selling a lifestyle. With revenues of more than $1 billion, the company spends a little less than $2 million a year on advertising. The company also encourages events such as the annual Harley Toys for Tots ride through Martha's Vineyard and other locations.

Was the evolution of Harley a conscious plan from the beginning? Probably not. But they are certainly aware of where their brand lives now, and they nurture that with everything they have. Yes, they know where their brand lives, and that wouldn't be Harley headquarters, they know it lives at its best in the riders, out on the open road. Their goal is to keep it all fresh and in step with technological innovation, yet still traditional in look and feel.

The Living Nature of a Brand

A number of brands have taken on a life of their own, like a batch of sourdough mix—bubbling and alive. Managers of the brand have either learned to roll with that, to adjust and go with the flow, to make something of the best of all that, or have stumbled and the brands have languished or disappeared. When Ivy League students decided it was "camp" to start wearing the rubber-soled boots and rough outdoorsy jackets of sporting good companies like L.L. Bean and Abercrombie & Fitch, it didn't take long for those firms to see the light and exchange limping sales in trout flies and snowshoes for the market support of the customer group with the most disposable income who wanted to join "the club."

What is going to become extremely important for your company is the role of what's been labeled the brand manager. It's basically the person who holds the keys to the quality of customer experience, of what people see and feel and interact with. A recurring theme in this book is that you need to design your process and infrastructure around what your end user sees and feels and experiences, and then go out and make sure your system supports all this. It gets more and more complicated as you're developing a product and your design is done in San Francisco, and your engineering is done in Taipei, your manufacturing is done by another company in China, there's yet another company providing the packaging, and then someone else is doing the logistics, and so on.

In this expanded role, a new skill set has to develop where an individual or individuals are really chartered with holding, protecting, and developing that experience, and always making sure to remember that your customer doesn't care about your supply chain, doesn't care how sophisticated or how well-leveraged you are. The customers care about what they want. And what they want is a great experience of feeling more alive. If wearing an Abercrombie & Fitch hooded sweatshirt that costs three times as much as the one they can get at Wal-Mart makes them feel more like they belong to their peer group, so be it. The gut has spoken.

A new skill set has to develop for the "brand manager" where there are really chartered with holding and developing the overall customer experience.

Your Brand Communicates

Brand and branding, for the most part, are really overused terms, and by many people they are completely misunderstood. When you say brand, too many people think logo, think about what their advertising is, what their corporate identity looks like, or what their packaging or retail presence looks like. Worse, some get caught up in what their competitors are saying and how their product or service fits when compared against that. When we started working with MasterCard over a decade ago, they were obsessed with what Visa was up to. You get in that kind of mindset and right away you start doing a lot of externally focused stuff instead of listening to the dialogue between the product and the customer. MasterCard began a new dialogue about what business they were in. The comment got made that while you can't use your MasterCard to buy happiness, you can use it for most everything else. This lead to the Priceless campaign. MasterCard repositioned the brand as a portal to "priceless" experiences. The rest as they say, is history.

It begins with dialogue (fr. Gk dialogos: *flow of meaning*). Listen in, for example, and see if you can hear the promise Apple makes to the customer, because, believe us, that's the beginning of the journey for an established successful brand. It starts with a promise that has meaning to the customer. And it is a promise that must be kept.

When you first see pictures of an iPhone, it starts giving you information. When you read about it, you get more information. As soon as ads start appearing, you get more information. When you first look at and touch it, you add to all you have gathered. If you buy it and experience how it works, you've added still more—to what you were able to gather; you have added personal-level emotional experience to the mix. With all this, you have been building up an idea of what the iPhone is and what it might mean to you. Before you ever bought it, you had a certain context of expectations. You emotionally prequalified the product before purchase. Now that you own it, it's up to the brand to keep the promise.

Courtesy of Apple Inc.

That promise starts when you first hear the word *Apple* or see the logo and you maybe think: "Gee, the Mac is easy to use. Everyone acknowledges that, even PC owners. I've had good experiences with my iPod. And that time I had to return an Apple product, I had a good experience. So I might just give this iPhone a chance. But don't you let me down." So they—the product and the customer—are already communicating and seem to be getting along. It's starting to look like it's up to Apple to deliver on the promise, or else betray the promise. According to Job's, the dialogue at Apple went something like this: "We all had cell phones. We just hated them; they were so awful to use. The software was terrible. The hardware wasn't very good. We talked to our friends, and they all hated their cell phones too. This is a great challenge. Let's make a great phone that we fall in love with."

When your brand communicates well, you create a context of expectations. The product is emotionally prequalified before the purchase is made.

The logo and advertising have been part of what led toward a purchase decision, but it's the design experience of this and past products that makes or breaks the sale.

Apple's logo, through the years, has evolved from a kind of elaborate little doohickey of Newton sitting under a tree to the iconic rainbow apple with a bite taken out, to a more recent and sweeping metallic version. The evolution reflects that design has been a consistent part of Apple's interaction with its customer base (and didn't that rainbow suggest that at least once in his life Steve Jobs might have owned a tie-dyed T-shirt before his move to basic black). But, however stylish the logo has become, it isn't the brand in the larger sense—it is an iconic symbol of an experiential promise flowing from the design driven nature of Apple.

All you knew from or about Apple in the past amounted to an essentially Gestalt understanding, in that the total was more than the sum of the parts. Apple has leveraged your past experience as to whether you trust its products, or whether they have been designed for the sort of experience you expect will be positive. To this extent, when a new product is announced, it already has a jump ahead of everyone else in the space. Within months of release, the iPhone became the #2 player in the Smartphone space, way ahead of all the established players except the folks behind the BlackBerry. This ability to engender a dialogue and advance understanding comes through time and consistence, all the while being strategic about using design. This Gestalt is a capital asset. That's what few companies seem able to get; this idea. Why? Because, once again, it isn't Excel friendly. It is, to some degree, abstract; certainly emotional. It's about the human experience. It's about things you have to do that you can't measure. You have to have faith that this is, in fact, important, and you have to trust your instincts. These are all things that go into the commitment to design a design driven culture.

What often happens is the manager needs to justify a proposal to the vice president, and the vice president needs to justify that to the president, and the president needs to justify that to the board. Unless they're all comfortable and believe they can monetize a positive customer emotional experience, they struggle. It's a struggle to go in front of the board and say: "This emotional stuff is really important and we've got to spend a hundred million dollars on this." If everyone up and down the line doesn't fundamentally believe and understand, it's a challenging thing to get done.

There are scenarios where people have had some success, and they're smart enough to realize how design was the successful component and they begin to build on it. Then there are a whole lot of people who can't seem to get their arms around the idea that you need to invest in being design driven beyond a one-time deal. The vast majority of companies that are developing products view the design component as a step in the process. You lay out the product development timeline. You go through the steps to identify an opportunity. You research the opportunity, develop ideas, engineer, manufacture, distribute, and promote. Design kind of happens somewhere in the development of the idea, and design might happen in the promotion space of advertising and packaging and things like that. Design, in these contexts, is a mere event or a series of discrete events in a discrete process, which aren't integrated into the soul of the company. When you make the shift to an integrated design experience that permeates all aspects of your company's development, manufacturing, delivery, and follow-up flows, you end up with a far stronger brand.

The vast majority of companies that are developing products view design as a step in the process, not the driving factor.

What matters about a brand is an individual's gut feeling. When a bunch of individuals have the same gut feeling, you have a brand.

That's because brand isn't about all the external aspects, and it's not at the whim of what your competitor is up to. It lives as an individual feeling in the gut of your customer, because we all make up our own version of your brand—your brand lives in our bellies. Everyone makes their own decision about what a company's brand is and what it means and what they feel about it. That's the way it is because that's the way we are, that's the way people operate. What matters is an individual's gut feeling.

When a bunch of individuals have the same gut feeling, you have a brand. It's not what *you* say it is; it's what *they* say it is.

Oops! Lost It There for a Second

The brand consistently named the number-one brand nationally and internationally is Coca Cola. So, how was it that the company in 1985 lost its eye on the prize by introducing New Coke, a move that threatened to jeopardize the brand. The perception that the brand was losing ground to Pepsi—at the end of World War II, Coke had 60 percent of the market, and that had shrunk to 23 percent by 1983—led to the "Project Kansas" market research that indicated a sweeter coke did well in the kind of taste tests Pepsi was featuring in its commercials. It was a honeymoon destined to end in a brawl, and three months later the original Coke was back as Classic Coke, eventually to become just Coca Cola again as New Coke faded into the sunset. This is an old story. But as it relates to staying true to your own design focus and ignoring external aspects, it's, well, a classic!

Your Brand Is About Value

A good design-savvy company is also cognizant of value. Value doesn't always equate with a product or service being the least expensive. It's about the customer getting a satisfying experience for the money, whether from a cup of coffee, an electronic device that is functional and fun, or a service that is always dependable.

One of the challenges is figuring out what people really value and what they are willing to pay for. That's where Apple pays attention. Typically, they're slightly above the industry in price. But it's not an issue because people see the value; they're getting a higher-quality product; they're getting a better experience; they're getting the Apple brand and associations that come with the Apple brand for that extra bit of money spent.

Remember being in the Apple Store back in Chapter 2, "Do You Matter"—when on the way out, you buy a wall charger for your iPod for $29.95, and even if you know you can get a DVD player for less than that at Best Buy, it doesn't seem to bother you? So you toss it into your basket and you still feel good, even if you paid a little more than the going rate for wall chargers. Or maybe you've been on eBay, where you looked at the going rate for a used MacBook Pro versus a Dell or an HP equivalent. You see that a MacBook Pro commands a significant price premium. Then you remember the cool, free, non-Microsoft software that comes with every Mac, so you're thinking, "Well, the Mac just works, and when it's all added up, it might actually cost less."

Here is another glimpse of the economic value of designing a brand experience. Although it's something that's really tough to define and equate in absolute terms, the described scenarios underscore how a company's brand is their most valuable asset.

In contrast, consider again a company such as Motorola, traditionally possessed of a strong engineering oriented culture. That in itself isn't enough to catch the customer experience, especially when they are trying at the same time to be cool. It doesn't matter if they end up proclaiming after the features, benefits, and techno speak: "And we're really cool." It doesn't matter what they say if people don't feel it. You can't tell people what to feel with your brand. They're going to come to their own conclusions in spite of what you pitch or spin. Take a product like the Razr. It ends up being a major blip instead of a trend. Why? Because, even if they have ads that say, "Hello, Moto," it's still like, "Oh, no, that's Motorola there, that geeky little symbol. That's really who they are."

What matters is what people think and feel about your brand. And you don't control that. While you cannot control what people feel, what you must do is provide influence, and make sure that how you're doing this authentically represents who you are and what you offer.

How To Really Be Cool, Not Just Act Cool

Imagine taking on one of the biggest market segments in the world, where the output of established competitors is in the billions of units. Your competitors have a firm hold on the major distribution channels, and their advertising budgets are in the mega-millions. Yet you do it without any advertising. Sounds like a gnat on the hip of an elephant, right?

With a motto of "Run with the little guy... create some change," Peter van Stolk of Seattle began what was to become the Jones Soda Company in 1987, though he had never gone to college or studied marketing. The first thing he did was learn the rules of the bottled soda market so he could ignore them.

He competed against companies so big they risked losing touch with the experience of their consumers. Stolk went right to consumers and invited them to put their own pictures on his beverage labels. Initially from a web site that encouraged people to get involved by submitting photos from which a few were selected to be put on the products, Jones Soda evolved to a social network eager to exchange the ever-changing labels in web chat rooms, and then provided an opportunity for those eager to bypass the selection process by getting their own pictures on the labels when they ordered more than 12 bottles.

Of course, the quickest category of consumers to have this approach tickle their fancy was that of those aged 12 to 24, the fastest growing segment, with more than 50 million prospective customers. To that target audience, flavors like Crushed Melon, Fufu Berry, Green Apple, Bug Juice, and Bubble Gum, all in bright neon colors, have a huge and hip appeal. (One Thanksgiving, the company sold 6,000 bottles of turkey and gravy soda.) To appeal to the health food savvy, the company recently moved away from corn syrup to pure cane sugar as their ingredient for

sweetness. The main source of buzz is through social media interaction. Quick to tap the subculture interest in urban wonders like "what happens when you put Mentos in Diet Coke" (don't try this at home, by the way), you can go to YouTube and see a video "Jones Soda and the Mentos Experiment." The company's photos and videos emphasize sports such as skateboarding, extreme sports, the wacky, and the weird.

Without a look back or sideways to his competitors, Stolk is already bringing in $40 million a year in revenue, and he owes it all to consumer involvement. Jones's customers feel like they've joined something. As he puts it, "When you're marketing without money, you have to stay true to the fact that you need to make an emotional connection." You might say "Well—it's only $40 million in annual revenues"—but if you owned it, how good would that be?

Your Brand Should Be As Alive As a Person

Another way to look at brand is that it is like an individual's character. *That's really what a brand is, the embodiment of a company's character.* When you think of the character of people, you find things about them that encourage you to like or dislike them. When you first meet someone, you might draw a few conclusions based on how they dress and style their hair, and few more of their mannerisms. A lot of times you're right, and a lot of times you're not. But then, as you gain real insight into their ethics and values and how they treat others, you begin to understand the person's character. That's how you really

Character is built on ethics, on behavior, how people treat others, and how they treat you, and that's how you build an idea of who they are. It's the same thing with a brand.

start to define how you feel about somebody. It's the same way with a company.

You can dress up people in cool clothes, and give them a hip new hairstyle, and create some ideas about, "Wow, maybe they're really pretty cool and hip," but as you really start to get to know them, you realize that, "No, they're really moving violations of the truth in packaging laws." All this is a veneer. You start to wonder about them. It's the same thing with companies. It's sort of, "Would the real character please stand up?" And character is built more on ethics, on behavior, how people treat others, and how they treat you, and that's how you build an idea of the character of each of them. It's the same thing with a brand. That's exactly what you need to do; communicate at a gut level and have people to get to know your company's character through all the authentic things they experience. That comes back to the overall experience, and that's what is so important to a brand.

The big mistake a lot of marketers make is to think, "OK, we need our brand to be cooler. So let's make our brand cooler, and we'll tell people we're cooler, and they'll have to think we're cooler." But if it's not in your character, it's a mistake. A company really needs to build the qualities of who they are—their purpose, their vision, and their values—they need to be authentic. So, if you are, for example, Motorola, and you need to be more hip and modern, and you need to communicate this to people, then you need to actually *become* more hip and modern. You can't just create some ads that do that; you really have to start to look at how are you operating, how are you making decisions, what do you care about, and start to change those things. That takes time, and it's important.

Your brand lives in your customer's heart. You can only influence it.

Being cool is a lot easier if you are, in fact, cool. Take the new audio brand Beats by Dr. Dre. As the recording industry redefines itself to adjust to the idiosyncrasies of digital downloads, companies and artists are looking for new ways to leverage their equity in the marketplace. One way is to market products under a celebrity's name, and while this is not new in clothing and fragrances, developing "celebrity" consumer electronics is a play not attempted until recently. The rap and hip-hop producer Dr. Dre and Intercope records Chairman Jimmy Iovine have formed an alliance with the design group

The Beats by Dr. Dre audio brand has been built on the idea of extending the producer's expertise and experience into the design.

Ammunition and manufacturer Monster cable to produce audio products, specifically high-quality headphones. The end result is an authentic product and brand that is tuned to the producer's sound, and designed to relate to his audience. The products are endorsed and worn by actual celebrities. The headphones are objects of lust and sound amazing. The brand does not have to try to be cool. It is cool. And it is authentic.

Brand and experience—it's like the Queen Mary. The turns are big and take a lot of time and a lot of momentum to happen. As with a person, once you've decided somebody's an ass, it's going to take you a little while, and some experience, to turn that around, even if you happen to be motivated to do so. Just talking to them once in a while won't do it. You're going to have to work with them a while, and be with them, give them a chance, before you decide, "Well, maybe they're not so bad. Maybe they're OK." It's the same thing with a company. Once you've decided they don't deserve the negative values you've created about them in your gut, you might become a customer again. But it takes time—they need to prove it to you, and you need to give it a chance. With a company, that often doesn't happen because the disenchanted customer doesn't need to make the effort, and usually won't.

Once There, a Brand's Success Is Yours to Lose

When you've made it, established a brand people like and respect, nothing can touch you. Right?

Is that right, Levi-Strauss? Nodding your head, Polaroid? One of the great American Tragedies is the list of companies once successful that are now in their declining days, if not already put to rest in a corporate coffin with a lily on the chest. The fact is, you are not going to make everyone happy, but once you energize your customers against you and start to see web sites like www.ihatestarbucks.com, then you know there is trouble in River City.

One sure sign a company is headed down a slippery slope is when the new CEO doesn't focus first on customer experience as the basis for the design of everything. When Phil Schoonover took over as CEO of Circuit City Stores, Inc. in 2006, one initial step was to save the company back into profitability. In 2007, he cut 3,000 workers as part of an initiative to save $200 million a year. At the same time, he said, "We want engaged associates who have fun at work, bring a passion about the products, and enjoy serving customers."[17] He wanted, he said, for the company to become an employer of choice. Really? Handing out pink slips sure fires up the joy machine. Right? Well, that does still leave the company with 43,000 employees. But employees are "customers" too. How's their experience doing?

More to the point, the move signals his first eye isn't on the company's design to effectively drive an enhanced customer experience, but rather on employee costs, prices, and other externals.

How has this worked out? Well, the buzzards are watching with eager anticipation.

Another interesting scenario to follow will be what Lenovo does to the IBM ThinkPad, which is a great notebook brand, now that Lenovo has acquired the IBM PC Group. The ThinkPad has been an iconic brand in its market segment, and what happens next will depend on whether Lenovo, which is known for low price-point machines, will really understand what was important about the ThinkPad experience. Within a few years, one possibility is that it's just going to be another notebook built by an Asian company. If that's the case, they will have squandered what they paid for the equity of the brand. It's theirs to keep and prosper from, or to lose.

How Do You Know How You're Doing in Respect to Customer Experience?

One of the hardest things for you to see is yourself from the perspective of others. The same goes for companies. They might be aware of the need for a shift in awareness, and they might have the determination to do it right, but it's by no means a given. Younger companies, on the order of Jones Soda, seem to get it quite clearly sometimes. While for more established companies, it can be a real struggle. *It's typical for a lot of large companies to sense they are in trouble, but not know why.* For those companies, it's wise to bring in professional help, to hire a design consultant, or add staff with that skill. They need help understanding how their design experience and brand is degraded, and how they can change that.

One of the biggest challenges that designers face is business credibility. When you slip on your

CEO (that would be chief experience officer) cap and look hard at your company, it's usually difficult to envision making a sweeping, systemic change from one end to the other. The common tendency is to want to put just one toe in the water, to try this one thing. We'll tell a company they can hire us to design a product, to get to know them, to look at the product line, and we sometimes have to say, "Look, your overall experience is off. You need to do something about that. You need to rethink how you present yourself to people." And they respond with, "Yeah, yeah, but you're a designer. We hired you to help our engineers develop a product, and we respect you for that, but you're talking about stuff you don't know about."

There is still a gap in business culture, at least American business culture, of really viewing design as a business partner.

That's why there is still a credibility gap in business culture, at least in American business culture, of really viewing design as a business partner. When a designer with the experience and talent looks at what you're doing and says, "You're missing it, you're not doing it right, and you're not communicating appropriately," there's still an undercurrent of, "Yeah, yeah. I know. But what do you know; you don't have an MBA." That's the more hidebound established perspectives of those who are dead right, right up to the point they disappear. Many younger start-up companies these days are more willing to engage. They're really thinking about: "What are we doing?" One good example of that is Slingbox. They've done a lot of things right in defining who they are through their brand, and in their design experience.

It's a tough concept too, if you think about it. One of the chief foes of a new product and how

© Sling Media, Inc.

The Slingbox is an iconic design, but that is just part of it. Its brand is about delivering a valuable service that is really well thought-out and defined.

it can connect to a customer experience is the uphill fight against inertia, against whatever is already established. Slingbox's entry to market involved that sort of "location shifting," of being able to have a TV at home and then slinging the content up on the internet and being able to view it on a laptop or a mobile phone from virtually anywhere on earth. They've done a pretty good job of making people see the value in this along with the experience of the product; it works really well. The little boxes are iconic, and that's part of it, but the whole set up and operation, and what it is and how it works and what it's delivering, is really well thought-out and well defined. It's a lot easier when you're a start-up and you're starting fresh to do that. Like we said, it's much harder to go back and change things that are already in place, especially if they've been in place for years and years and years.

For a CEO of an established company, once things start to go wrong, and it's painfully, publicly obvious that it's gone wrong, the road back is very difficult. Just like the human body, or the family auto, your company needs an annual checkup. What companies should do is not just fret about their specific needs to develop a product, but audit what they're doing overall and how they're presenting themselves to the public. The time-established ways of marking and measuring how they are doing aren't going to cut it when it comes to customer experience. Just because you've gotten customer surveys and employee surveys, you still haven't gotten to the gut level. Our experience is that most executives are not very good at relating what they find in those surveys to the totality of their culture, and what those surveys are the early warning signals for. They're not able to contextualize the information in ways that make it actionable.

Sometimes—especially in surveys out to the general public—you have to view the feedback contextually. The person that's giving the information might have special circumstances. You can see obvious trends but few people are equipped to figure out what gut feelings you're creating in people. You probably need to hire people who understand design to look at why and how your customers are getting the feelings they do. What is it that you're doing throughout your customer experience supply chain that's creating the bad brand experience for people? You also need to be really clear about what you're doing really well so you can do more of it.

The idea of having an annual audit is a good thing. Saying every year you will look at how you're performing, and maybe where to start is to define the things to measure. But what are the things you should be auditing?

In the world of operations, a lot of companies have tons of ways of measuring the things they know and can quantify. Dell is extraordinarily adept at measuring stuff. What most companies don't know, though, is how to measure, really get a hands-on grasp for, customer experience. They might admit, "OK, I understand it matters; now, how do I actually measure it?" How do I get insight into it, what are the right metrics?" The fact is, there aren't clear metrics, and if you try to do it too often, you actually hurt the situation. Some of it is a leap of faith, and there you either need to develop the razor-edge instincts of a consumer—and we think Apple has done that—or

What most companies don't know is how to measure and really get a hands-on grasp for customer experience.

you need to hire talent, inside or outside, to help you develop a culture that is able to do all this. You need to believe that design matters, you need to believe that experience is important, and then you need to look at the things that create great experience. We are talking about emotional reality here, and you can't put emotions on a spreadsheet.

In the next chapter, to support what you've considered here, you explore how products can become portals to experience that matter to customers, along with how you design for experience chain management.

Products As Portals

Products as portals to experiences that matter to customers—designing a great experience with a consistent promise across multiple touch points—how you use design for customer experience supply chain management.

You are CEO of a company with 50,000 employees, and you are so dedicated to the concept of customer experience driving the quality and value of your household products that in 1985, when a line of your company's refrigerators were found to be defective, you had the workers who'd made them line up and smash 76 of them to smithereens. Hell, you grabbed a sledgehammer and smashed away at one of the damned things yourself. The public smashing of products that don't make the cut appears to be somewhat *de rigueur* for Pacific Rim companies. You have been recognized by *Financial Times* as a turnaround specialist, and your company's brand philosophy is "Be brand the sail, be customer the teacher." Well, your intentions are good.

So what happens when you go on the Internet to a site, www1.shopping.com,[18] and you look at 25 reviews of a product you released, a Haier XQG65-11SU Front Load All-in-One Washer/Dryer, and the reviews read:

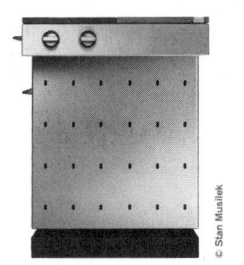
© Stan Musilek

- Worst product, worst experience ever! Do not ever buy a Haier product.

- I'm a lemon. Do not buy this or any Haier washer/dryer combo unit.

- CUSTOMER SERVICE STINKS!

- Badly engineered, unreliable.

- The poor quality is mind-boggling. A piece of junk.

This goes on and on like this, until, if you're on a plane, you reach for the barf bag. Your name is Zhang Ruimin, chairman and chief executive officer of Haier, and you're not having your best day. You reach for your cell phone and start seeing what you can do about damage control.

All around the globe there are well-intentioned CEOs like Zhang Ruimin who do everything they can to seek excellence and drive that by listening to customers. You can talk the talk and seek to walk the walk, but the bigger your company is, the harder it is to ensure that every single thing goes according to plan. Therein lies the rub.

You live and die based on the emotions of customer experience, but once they grab the torches and pitchforks and begin to storm the castle, *all* your products are imperiled. If you are Zhang Ruimin, you hope you can put out this brushfire before it spreads. You have other products where the reviews are much better. Just how much has this one mess prejudiced the buying public?

As noted before, the consumer horde can be somewhat forgiving if a brand it has grown to trust stumbles now and again. But, as with Tylenol or, in this case, Haier, quick and healing action is vital if you are to smooth the overall sense of customer experience as it relates to your product. In a larger sense, it is the task of any company that wants to be truly design-driven to watch the customer experience meter as if it is the barometer of your survival, and in many cases it is.

How do you let customer experience drive and permeate every aspect of your total company and all products or services, no matter how big or small your company might be? That is what we intend to explore.

Starting with Experience, Hopefully Ending with It

Richard Branson, Virgin Airlines, says, "I started an airline because the experience of flying on other airlines was such a miserable experience."

The driving force behind the design idea of the inception of many companies had to do with customer experience. Edwin Land invented the Polaroid camera after his daughter asked, "Why can't we look at the pictures right away?" The idea was good, at first. More than fifty years later, it could well have been made into a song to play at Polaroid's funeral, with the photos being taken with digital (instant) cameras.

Getting how important experience is, and keeping that notion, is as vital to doing business for a design driven company as anything you can grasp. Sometimes you can orchestrate everything to go your way. Other times you might

It is the task of any company that truly wants to be design-driven to watch the customer experience meter as the barometer of its survival.

need to go at the mission like riding a bucking bronco. The choice is up to you to do as much as you can up front, and that's not so easy or *PCWorld* wouldn't have a list of "The 25 Worst Tech Products of all Time."[19]

When the public is sorting through the good, the bad, and the ugly of products or services, you know where you want to be. But how can you ensure you don't stumble? Well, the fact is there is no one person or company with a perfect record in everything. There are examples, though, where there is a consistent aim to use customer experience to drive the design of products or services, and though focus groups and research are often used, they aren't as effective as getting and staying on a gut-on-gut basis with customers.

Although not easy to do, at the same time not as hard as you might think, because we all have our own personal experience as a touchstone. There is a silly line in the old but still funny classic movie *Caddyshack* where Chevy Chase gives golf advice by chanting the mantra: "Be the ball. Be the ball." Well, it's not so silly when you start aiming to "Be the customer. Be the customer." That's certainly how Steve Jobs is thinking when he is muttering, "Hey, I can't use these damned buttons." Or, "I can't read from this screen. We need to fix that." You need to know your customer. Jobs knows his very well and stays focused on this. The Apple customer is narrow, but aspirational. It is why the iPod crossed over and you see members of the older generations with iPods.

But even Steve Jobs, or any person or company mentioned in this book, must keep fresh with that—constantly relearn and reapply and reexperience the world of the customer or take the fall from good to bad or ugly. It's a constant, living approach for a business, and that's why it's a chore to get there, or stay there. You can do this. CEO or not, the power of one person to make a difference is real.

Being the Customer

Take a company like THX. If you have been in a movie theater anytime lately, you have felt the company's signature sound dopple in one of your ears through your head and out the other side. What a nice way to "show" how they work too, instead of just "tell." The company does more than just certify the sound in theaters. As *CE Pro* put it, "If there's one electronics logo that consumers across the world recognize, it's THX. They see it on their favorite DVDs, electronic equipment, and even video games."[20] When the company is mentioned in relation to a product or venue, you expect a good experience. In a quite Pavlovian way, you are drooling for a rich sound happening.

Stop and think about this: George Lucas is a filmmaker who was motivated by having to endure a crappy audio rendition of his work in the theater, so he gets involved all the way to the delivery of his product to the public.

The company began in the early 1980s when George Lucas was not happy with the consistency of sound in theaters. He was working on the third of his *Star Wars* films, *Return of the Jedi*, and had put a lot of effort into the special effects, including sound, and didn't want that work to be wasted. Stop and think about that for the moment. He's a filmmaker, who should just be making movies, but he is motivated by having endured in a theater or two where he had a crappy audio experience, so he gets involved all the way to the delivery level of his product to the public.

THX was developed by Tomlinson Holman at the Lucasfilm company site, and THX, Ltd. (www.thx.com) has not rested on its initial laurel. The THX II Certified Car Audio System was recognized as one of the Best Car Audio Systems of 2006 by the editors of CNET. The company is expanding to home video systems and training programs, and in every instance, it begins with sitting down in the customer's chair and getting inside that customer's head.

Follow this sequence: THX started with the idea of ensuring moviegoers with a terrific auditory experience. They built the brand within theater promotional spots placed before the main feature. As people began to connect the brand to the pleasure of great sound, THX started making the experience portable, out of theaters into homes and cars by way of THX certified components, including headphones. The brand is now perceived by people as a portal to a more rewarding entertainment experience.

How Do You Do This?

Let's say you start with a personal experience you think could be improved, made current, or even approached from a different direction and you say, "We're going to design a superior customer experience; that's the starting point." Then you design an organization to design the product or service and deliver the experience. That's what Cirque du Soleil did.

It's what Alice Waters did when she got the idea for Chez Panisse, which has been rated the #1 restaurant in America by *Gourmet* magazine and consistently stays near the top of their list. She was nominated as one of the ten most important people in food by the French, and she's *American*. It all started for her when, as a student at U.C. Berkeley, she spent a year abroad and got immersed in the culture of Paris and Provence. There she came to understand how food is really about the experience of the community gathered around the table, and that while the food should at least be good, the experience extends from the local growers, enhanced by culinary skills to the pleasures of the table and good companionship. In this tradition, you couldn't say "what's for dinner" until you discovered what was available fresh that day when you went to market. That became the experience Alice wanted to consistently offer through her restaurant Chez Panisse in Berkeley, which opened its doors in 1971. How has this worked out? Almost four decades of brilliance to date.

That was how Howard Schultz's head was working when he visited Milan and said, "This is an experience coffee customers would be willing to pay a little more to share." Both Alice Waters and Howard Schultz were CEOs of their companies in the sense that they were chief experience officers in the conception of their businesses. Schultz arrived at the Starbucks experience. How brilliant was that? Well, in retrospect it seems one of those things that's incredibly obvious, but what a few other people probably realized, namely that the coffee shop was about more than getting coffee, Schultz and Starbucks implemented brilliantly. Schultz didn't think he was in the coffee business, he was in the experience business, and the portal into that experience was a better cup of coffee in a carefully designed atmosphere. We are reminded of our favorite Mae West line here; "I used to be Snow White and then I drifted." Starbucks has drifted. It remains to be seen if they can rebuild the experience and survive commoditization.

Portals to Experience

Really well-designed products or services become an icon and a venue, a doorway or portal for a specific community to a unique experience.

In the *Harry Potter* books and movies, there are magical ways to get around for wizards, and one is by way of a portal. If you touch it, you are whisked away to a far-away place; the other end of the connection. That's how really well-designed products or services work: The product becomes an icon and a venue, a doorway or a portal for a specific community to a unique experience, and that's where you start to create equity.

Even a thing like a book is a portal. Don't think of this thing you hold in your hands as a product. Look at it as a portal. If it is a success at sharing the importance of valuing customer experience and using that as you design your organization (even if that's you at home in your pajamas as you launch your startup) and products or services, then it has swept you through and on to a better place.

A product or service can equally be the portal to a negative customer experience. If your knees are jammed into your face and the flight attendant is carrying some serious attitude and if you're late and miss a connection and making a new one is a huge hassle, and then your luggage turns up missing and customer service is an oxymoron, then you have not been flying Southwest or Virgin—you've been flying a legacy airline. Well, let's be fair—being a legacy airline in the current environment is an extraordinarily challenging place to be. And any airline can take a pop when weather shifts or security at airports is tightened, or any number of things that can go wrong do go wrong.

But how they handle all this and keep you moving with a smile on your face nevertheless all comes down to whether their airline has been sustained as a portal to a good experience or has drifted to become a gateway to misery and frustration. It all loops back to: "Do they start with how a customer feels?" You can retain the services of one of the world's great design firms (United did this), but if this is approached as a bolt on retrofit, like new overhead bins in an aging fleet, then all that happens is that misery gets to be better looking.

Do they design the customer experience supply chain so you don't end up with a grumpy flight attendant (this alone requires a carrier to relate to their people as if they were also customers—because airline crews want what the traveling public wants—a good experience) or seating that has ergonomically sacrificed your ability to ever walk upright again. Do they coordinate all the factors they can control toward being a positive part of your travel experience? Is everyone trained to make your flight consistently impeccable? And, if things go south because of some condition or event, are they are also prepared to make it right, quickly, and pleasantly? That doesn't always seem to happen with some companies, while it does with others. Customers notice. You probably have noticed, and it affects your decision process the next time

you are making travel plans. You find yourself
skipping over some better deals on "Air Misery"
to pay a bit more for an experience you can live
with, maybe even enjoy.

Don't play the game, change the game. Look to design to uncover new territory.

We acknowledge that it's hard to be United
or American, for example. It is incredibly difficult for a major legacy carrier to pull off an
extreme makeover. It is much easier to be
Southwest or Virgin Atlantic, because you had
the chance to design and build the culture from
scratch to deliver the experience you wanted
your chosen customers to enjoy.

Let's talk about grilling for a moment. That
a grill is a grill is a grill doesn't hold up anymore.

Not when someone has designed and built a barbeque grill expressly as a portal to the ultimate grilling experience. Enter the Fuego grill on which the food buzz is: "A beautiful grill that is being dubbed 'the iPhone of Grills.' This sure beats our 3-year-old George Foreman grill that resembles a first-generation iMac."[21] According to *ID* Magazine, "Fuego is an architectural reinvention of outdoor grilling. No mountainous hoods. No lumbering curves. Just streamlined functionality that puts modern design on the front burner."

As Sara Hart on *Dwell Dailey's* Tech Blog put it:

> *When a ubiquitous product gets a major upgrade, its packaging should separate it from its competitors. Fuego, North America, a San Francisco-based high-end home product firm, did just that when it created the Fuego Grill, an outdoor grill unlike any other. Its sleek, compact, stainless-steel body with teak countertops says, "I am not your daddy's Weber." The Quick-Change Drawer System allows the cooking method to be changed from gas to gas-fired infrared to traditional charcoal by simply swapping the drawers. It has a grill-surface temperature thermometer to gauge cooking time, and a modular system to accommodate all sorts of accessories, including a deep fryer, cast-iron griddle, wok, and steamer. The hood retracts completely out of the way. It won iF [magazine's] 2007 Product Design Award and was a winner in ID Magazine's 53rd Annual Design Review and most notably*

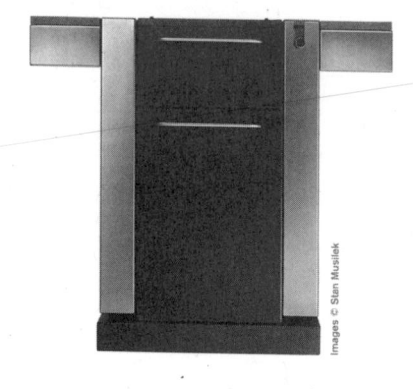

the 2007 IDEA Gold Medal for consumer products from BusinessWeek. *The Fuego 02 is a smaller version. The larger model sells for about $3,500.*[22]

So, how is one barbeque grill a portal to a better experience than another? Fuego understood and started with a dialogue on the idea that the barbeque is more than a cooking appliance. It is a hub for outdoor entertaining. The realization that the most common design of the barbeque, with the big hood, was actually an impediment to socialization, because it creates a dynamic where it's difficult to stand around, was nothing short of brilliant. Basically, with the legacy hooded grill, if you're cooking, everybody's behind you. You want to get into situations where you're cooking and everyone's around you. That was really the inspiration for the Fuego Grill, the understanding it's about a social experience. Fuego is more than just a cool grill that works really well; it is a portal to a richer outdoor social experience in a very modern way.

This All Sounds Good, But One More Time, How Do I Go About Doing It?

To some extent, all the things we've been discussing might seem a product of common sense. Think like a customer and always keep that in mind. This requires an unrelenting vigilance if you are to pull it off. When you try to do something in a big company, it becomes much harder to do. It takes a lot for Steve Jobs to throw himself into iPod design and ensure that every stage, from idea to delivery to customer to follow-up, all work. It also takes a team of amazingly talented people working together with a shared commitment to change the game forever. This represents the metaphorical equivalent of Roger Banister breaking the four minute mile. Once Banister did it in May of 1954, others followed. Banister's performance became the portal for other athletes. When you study the performance of the "Banisters of Business" focus on the ideas, do not get stuck in the weeds of so-called "best practices" because they rarely translate to another (and therefore different) organizational culture.

It is one thing for George Lucas to realize that he can make the best movies, but the experience will be diminished unless the sound in theaters is outstanding. It is a very demanding thing to design, develop, and deliver the sound dynamics of THX. Now imagine how hard it is for someone like Zhang Ruimin, our protagonist at the opening of the chapter, whose company puts out hundreds of products every year. Things can go wrong, as they did with the washer/dryer mentioned. Then you are in a state of damage control instead of progressing forward. You can't batten down the hatches and dive, dive, dive. You've got to stay out there and nurture your customer base back to that level of trust that was the intended promise with each design.

Now, that was always hard enough in the past, but it is much harder today because of the media and interactivity of the internet, as Haier found out when a majority of reviewers decided to let their teeth show when chatting about their experiences with the washer/dryer. The transparency of customer experience today is far greater than it has ever been, in part because of the power and immediacy of product review *by customers*. Whole brands have nose-dived because of one product that was rushed to market and created problems that could not be corrected, all this in an atmosphere where products *must* be rushed to market. Again the moral of the story is that although you can (and must) engineer time out of the manufacturing and distribution links of the chain, taking time out of the design cycle can be risky business.

Add working quickly in an environment where customers can now bite back, along with all the other hurdles any product faces, and you have the reason that doing everything right is so important, and is so difficult. Doing it right means you work across a whole variety of organizations within and without your company. That requires a lot of alignment and focus and shared thinking. Plus you need to constantly learn and improve how you develop and implement your experience across all disciplines. Very few people in most companies have the power to ensure this happens. The CEO is usually the one who drives that, aligns the organization and suppliers and everyone else, and says, "This stuff matters. This is how we're going to do it. You're empowered to make this happen, and I'm going to hold you

The transparency of the customer experience today is far greater today than it has ever been, in part because of the power and immediacy of review by customers. Whole brands have nose-dived because of this.

accountable and responsible for everything that leads to the eventual customer experience."

Having said that, we now live in a world where a division of a global company is often bigger than the larger companies of yesterday. This being the case, if you run a division, or you are the product manager of a line, you can apply all this stuff and who knows, you might end up transforming the whole business. As they say, "there's nothing harder to stop than a trend." Start a trend.

Customer experience supply chain management starts with the end in mind—what the customer feels, sees, hears, and touches.

The idea to embrace, understand, and implement, once you are prepared to make the leap, is that of an "experience chain" management style. This works whether you are dealing with a product or service and is not just about either of those. Customer experience supply chain management starts with the end in mind— the customer's experience—and continues with the design of every aspect of the corporate culture and operations so as to choreograph a total design and delivery of every detail of that intended experience.

Nordstrom comes up a lot when you talk about the retail sector because the company has made an identity for itself by having good products and excellent customer experience. Rumor has it a clerk even took a tire back for a credit from a customer although the Nordstrom stores don't sell tires. But then you know that could have happened if you've ever been in a Nordstrom store. If you seem to know what you're up to and are just browsing and having a good time, you're left alone to enjoy. But if your brow furrows, and you start glancing up the aisles, a clerk appears as if on silent feet and you get help; not everyday help, but that over-the-top-yet-gracious kind of help. You want to get a red cashmere sweater for your niece. The clerk shows you one display, then walks you across the store into another department to show you something more hip for a younger person, and it just happens to be on special. You've mentioned gift, so the clerk whips into a back room and reappears with your purchase wrapped in a clever, different way that is going to make your niece sure feel special. Well, for that matter, so do you.

So, how does Nordstrom do it? Do they just hire well, have an excellent training program, or what? The fact is, being the way they are is a conscious part of the big design picture from one end of the company to the other. The buyer knows it. The clerk certainly knows it. And you can go to the bank on that the CEO knows it. But isn't this something everyone could do? Couldn't this approach be commoditized? Well, it could, but be reminded, if it was easy, everybody would be doing it.

You go into a Container Store and you'll see banners proclaiming it has been voted one of the greatest places for employees to work. Why is that important to your experience? You look around. Good stuff, but mostly just variations on the basic box. You could perhaps cobble together something like it yourself and save some money. Before you know it you're talking with one of the employees and seeing how you can turn a closet into something able to hold twice what you can now, and with sturdy dependable components someone is ready to stand behind. So you skip the D.I.Y. box idea and buy what you need and head home to reconstruct that closet.

Contrast the Nordstrom or Container Store experience with what happens when you go into Wal-Mart. A person greets you at the door, which shows they are making the effort. The clerks are all readily identified by a blue smock that says they are eager to help you. But the body language is often wrong and you overhear grumbling. What the heck! You're here for prices, aren't you? You put up with a vendor rep who is so busy stocking shelves you can't even get to a product you want, and the overhead PA system shoots you right out of your socks a couple of times, but at last you have what you came for, and you head for checkout. There are 20-item express lines that don't look to be moving all that fast. There's a place where you can check out your own goods (and you start thinking for an extra buck they might let you mop their floors). Then there are the usual checkout lines for people who seem to wait until everything in their house must be replaced all at once.

You have to bake customer experience supply chain management into every part of the culture. And you have to measure and reward people accordingly.

But here's something. When you were coming in you looked across and saw a bob of curly yellow hair on checkout row #9. That's Betty. You saw other people glancing to see if she was there too. When you get in that line, it is seven or eight carts long while other checkout rows only have two or three stuffed carts. But you're fine with waiting. Everyone in your row is smiling, and many chat to each other. Folks in the other rows are frowning, and look ready to bite. You finally get up to Betty who asks how you've been and she chats about her grandkids. The two of you have an authentic real person to real person kind of chat while you're there, and she's smiling and you are too as you leave.

Then you look around. Does the manager get what's going on here? No, he's standing over by an end cap talking with a couple of other employees, and he doesn't seem to pay any attention at all. He might walk by sometimes and think, "Got a good one there." But is it part of the store or chain's conscious effort to make more employees bond with customers? No. The company has several formalized pep rally approaches to make this happen, but if you're one of those employees not getting health benefits or who just took the job because it's the only place that would have you, or work in the meat department where the products are shipped in each day because someone tried to start a union once, chances are you leave any cheerfulness you have left at the door when you come in to work every day.

Point here is that you have to bake customer experience supply chain management into every part of the culture. And you have to measure and reward people accordingly. If they do not have the incentive to get the design and implementation right, it won't happen. So it needs to be a performance metric across the board. Everyone should have their impact to the customer experience defined and understood, metrics need to be developed, and people must be rewarded for achievement. Everyone.

Wal-Mart has an idea and is making an effort. They certainly have product supply side management down with respect to price, but you don't quite get the design quality you do at Target, and you most often don't even approach the service you get at a Nordstrom store. It's all about price, and when the wars begin, that isn't always going to be everything. You refer back to Sam Walton's "10 points" for his stores and you can see that he understood experience chain management.[23] The whole orchestration of what should be happening at each store is right there. But Wal-Mart is really only living up to one of those ten points, and that's the one about price, and it may well make them vulnerable. The rapid rise of Dollar General stores and others like it hint that the storm clouds are gathering.

Many of the things that worked once are going to be challenged going forward, and that's why you are going to need to be design driven if you are going to survive the change. We mentioned that the experience supply chain is one connecting continuum from customer experience all the way back to the beginning of the material supply chain. A reason that this whole idea of defining your customer experience, and building out how it's going to happen along all these links is harder now, is that the way it all happens today is very different than it was five, and especially ten, years ago.

What's changed is that there are so many entities involved. It used to be that companies really held very tightly to their supply chain and they wanted to design all their own materials, then develop all their own materials, and closely hold how they came to the system. So companies had a lot of infrastructure around development and manufacturing. That used to be how companies were successful—they really were great at that, they owned it, and it was proprietary.

The way it is today, you no longer own all the links in the chain. You have all these other companies that you contract with and bring in, you hire someone to manage the logistics, and it's all leveraged and outsourced. In that scenario, how do you maintain consistency? Or strategic consistency is a better term; you don't just want to be consistent, you want to be strategically consistent. How do you do that? You do that by defining very clearly what your customer experience is to be, the design language and everything else, and then have all your various partners and vendors comply to that and work to it. You run the risk of, by outsourcing so much, that you just end up with a hodgepodge of components. You have so many different viewpoints and methodologies coming into a process that in the end it can affect what the consumer sees. It's no longer something you know as well or even own, but still you have to manage it. Doing it all and doing it well and being consistent and vigilant about achieving and sustaining design integrity isn't easy.

The way it is today, you no longer own all the links in the chain. It's all leveraged and outsourced. In this scenario, how do you maintain consistency?

You Can Do It, We Can't Help

Let's look at an instance where the plan was good but someone threw a wrench into the working machinery. If you went into a Home Depot store when they first opened, you were greeted, directed to the aisle you wanted, and there you were met by an expert at what you wanted to do, whether find a paint to match or get a board trimmed so you can get back home and fix whatever it was that needed fixing. This was the experience design they built a store and a business around. Plus, of course, warehouse pricing.

Most of the floor representatives for each department were retired contractors or some other sort of experienced person who was able to really live up to the store's motto, "You can do it; we can help." In plumbing, you find a woman who surprises you by knowing more about pipes and fittings than you ever thought you wanted to know. You need to replace a toilet, you tell her, and you want to do it yourself, as you've heard can be done, to save a monster plumbing bill. She helps you figure out how much you want to spend and which fixture will best fit the space you have, and the next thing you know all the parts are loaded onto an oversized rolling cart and she's telling you exactly how to use the bee's wax seal that will have to be popped into place at the right time so you don't end up with a leak. You go home and you do it. That's how it was supposed to work, and that's how it did.

A few months later, you need to fix a PVC fitting, so you head to Home Depot. You know you need some kind of purple stuff and special glue and that there are elbows and such involved and you barely know what size of the white plastic pipe you're using. You have to find the section by yourself. It's now out by lumber, the last place you would have looked. You look around for help, get none. You ask a guy in an orange smock and he only works with wood and barely knows what a two by four is at that. So you go all the way inside to the plumbing department, looking for your plumbing angel, but she's gone. What the hell? When you do finally just go back, grab some stuff you hope will work, and head for a checkout counter, there's no one there. You have to ring up the items yourself, and that means looking a couple of them up on a chart. Steam is coming out of both ears and the "You Can Do It" stuff

Home Depot decided to save money by eliminating the more costly "area experts." Instead of saving money, the company went into a tail spin that not only lost a significant portion of its customer base, but also cost the company its supporting investors.

you're thinking about now involves the store manager and a wood chipper.

So, what happened here? The fact is, spreadsheet happened. When Bob Nardelli was Home Depot's CEO, the company decided to save money by eliminating the more costly area experts and also doing away with the ease of having a knowledgeable human being check you out. Instead of saving money, the company went into a tail spin that not only lost a significant portion of its customer base, but it also cost the company its supporting investors. One small step for Excel, one giant step for customer experience supply chain disaster. Didn't do much for Home Depot's stock price either.

Investment web sites were the first canaries to sense trouble in the coal mine. The Seeking Alpha web site's billboard read: "Home Depot: Should I Hold A Stock If My Customer Experience There Stinks?"[24] The web site of The Dividend Guy said, "It was probably the worst shopping experience I have ever had."[25] Think these are just ripples in the pond? Even Warren Buffet sold all his Home Depot stock.

The problem—once the pond was poisoned—permeated the entire customer experience chain. As Ohlin Associates put it: "No kinks revealed themselves more systematically or consistently than HD's externally managed rebates and warranty programs."[26] You only have to visit a few blog sites to see how widespread this annoyance had become.

It didn't take forever for Home Depot to wake up and spot the empty space where customers used to stand. Out went Nardelli and in came a new CEO, Frank Blake. He knew enough to go back to the secret sauce, being design driven around customer experience. But would it be enough? The folks at Ohlin tested his level of commitment and became believers that if anyone could make the turnaround, Frank Blake could. They said,

> "With scandal close behind and Lowes around the corner, HD is now acknowledging an eternal truth: that its huge capital investments require constant customer feeding and development across all levels of the organization. Customers are the lifeblood of any business. By paying attention not just to cutting costs through outsourcing and managing inventory better, but to the experiences of its customers, Frank Blake is building a culture that actively reaches out to you and me, telling us and showing us that Home Depot is putting every effort behind winning back your trust."[27]

What the W? A Hotel As Suite As They Come!

The W hotel chain has taken traveler experience to a new level in ways that only small boutique hotels had done in the past.

It is a comfortably warm Friday evening in June of 2001. Adam Campbell Smith and his wife Natalie get off a plane at La Guardia, head for baggage claim, and are relieved that their bags actually made it. So far so good. Natalie has Duke, their chihuahua in a carry-on satchel, and the three of them, along with the luggage, head across the Triborough Bridge in a cab bound for Manhattan and an experience they swear will be different this time. They'd had a budget one-week honeymoon in New York City years ago, and to celebrate a promotion and a twentieth wedding anniversary, they were returning to the Island from Iowa to do it right this time. A friend at work had given Adam the word that if he really wanted to do it right, he should pass on the Plaza and check in at the W. With some trepidation, Adam switched reservations. "What kind of hotel has a one-letter name?" he wondered. Still, when it came to romantic hotels, his friend was "the man."

And here they were, swept into a lobby that looks like someone's swank and very comfortable living room. They are greeted as if friends of the family. In the elevator, Natalie clears her throat and hopes she isn't getting a cold. Adam eyes a bottle of wine a bellhop is taking to another room. They are no sooner in their room, oohing and aahing over the natural tones of wood and nature, a bed that looks divinely inviting, and fixtures that make them feel they've moved into a new home and not a hotel, when the bell rings and at the door is a bellhop with a cart.

W Hotels has actually trained its staff to pick up on every clue to your experience and to respond to it.

"We didn't order anything," they say.

"I know," says the bellhop, delivering a bowl of chicken soup to soothe Natalie's throat along with a bottle of the wine Adam had been eyeing.

"How did they know?" Adam says. Natalie is gratefully tucking into her soup and Duke is exploring his W dog bed and has even found a doggie treat on his pillow.

"It's like they know what we want before we want it," Natalie says over her spoon. "Are we in the Twilight Zone?" she wonders out loud.

Here we have a hotel staff trained to pick up on every nuance of your body language as you go to your room, and one that responds by anticipating your needs. W Hotels has actually trained its staff to pick up on every clue to your experience and to respond to it. It could be spooky if you didn't end up feeling so pampered and special, which is just how you're supposed to feel at the W.

In the morning, Natalie is off to the hotel spa, Adam to the gym, and a staff member walks Duke in Central Park. How can you not love this kind of service? It is the kind of thing that won W Hotels one of FastCompany.com's 2005 Customers First Awards—that above and beyond sort of experience that can only be designed into a stay.

The operating sensibility that drove Sternlicht was, "Why should a visit to a hotel not feel like home?" He wanted an experience that was "like home, only better."

Ever been to a hotel and had a bad experience? Barry Sternlicht had, and the difference between him and a number of other disgruntled hotel patrons is that he decided to do something about it. He kept track of every pet peeve and used those to design a hotel experience that corrected every flaw.[28] The theme for his idea of a genuine feeling home away from home stay for weary travelers was something: welcoming, witty, warm, wonderful, whimsical, wow, and wired. Hence, the origin of the W Hotels, a line of quite stylish boutique suites, where each suite embodies and incorporates every function a traveler wants or needs, and then some.

As with Cirque du Soleil, the hotel chain sought to reinvent itself with every new hotel that opened. Like any design-driven enterprise, function was very much a part of form. What Sternlicht was after in every opening was a unique brand experience that was hip, fun, even exciting. He launched the W Hotels brand in 1998 with the original W Hotel in New York City, on 541 Lexington Avenue, followed with

one in Atlanta, and continued to expand through Los Angeles, San Francisco, Seattle, Mexico City, Seoul, Dallas, and Chicago, until there are more than thirty locations. But, to answer the quintessential question here: Why another hotel? What was so missing in the lineup for those who wish
to travel in style and comfort?

The operating sensibility that drove Sternlicht was, "Why should a visit to a hotel not feel like being at home?" He wanted an experience that was "like home, only better." He took a look at traditional hotels and saw pretty much the same old same old—an expectable sort of bedspreads and fixtures that screamed: "another night at a hotel." With all the quality products out there for the home, why should a hotel not take advantage. So the W Hotels went for designs that incorporate looks from nature for fresh looks quite unlike hotel rooms. The W beds are cloud-like layers of mattresses and feather beds with goose down duvets, just like Sternlicht had at home. He paid attention to every detail of lighting and design and behind it all sought to land on rooms that communicated that they were "cool and hip," not just comfortable. That meant oversized long desks, large TVs, and spacious bathrooms too. Wireless keyboards in every room, super-fluff towels, and over-sized shower heads all merge into a seamless sexier sort of place to stay. Even the lobbies of the hotels give the look and feel of a living room.

Sternlicht admitted that he had aimed to design class for mass, but ended up with a four-star brand, one that now offers lines of products that reflect and merchandise the W Hotel lifestyle. Other planned locations include

Athens, Istanbul, Doha, Dubai, Santiago, Hong Kong, and numerous sites around the globe. A part of Starwood Hotels and Resorts Worldwide, which has more than 860 hotels in more than 95 countries, W Hotels continue to prosper and grow, even though Sternlicht stepped down as CEO in 2004 to give his full attention to his other firm, Starwood Capital. The W Hotels weathered a tour as CEO by Steven J. Heyer, who was asked to step down by the Board because of management style issues and allegations of personal misconduct. As of September, 2007, Frits van Paasschen was appointed CEO of the W Hotel line.

The line continues to live up to its design-driven origins with unique offerings. For instance, everything is stylized in W Hotels; reception is referred to as "Welcome," the pool is "Wet." Just one of the unique promotions W Hotels has pioneered in recent years is "Woof." All five W Hotels in New York welcome canine guests with a doggy Signature W Bed, a doggy Bathrobe, a turndown treat, and doggysitting services that include walks through Central Park. If you reserve a Mega Suite at the W Seoul location, the Walkerhill, the hotel will have a red Jaguar waiting for you at the airport. W Hotels in Dallas, Chicago, Los Angeles, San Francisco, and New York all feature Bliss Spas.

Taking customer experience to a new level was enough to prove to the rest of the hotel industry that there is room for a fresh and inno-vative approach. For W Hotels to continue its growth along this experience design path will take all the things we've talked about. So far, most customers seem to agree that the experience is just plain "Wonderful."

That's really customer experience supply chain management in a nutshell. In the pages ahead, you'll look at ways to thoroughly understand and implement what we've been talking about. But think for a moment about this: How sweet could it be to start out right in the first place, or, if already started, not stumble and have to do everything all over again to make things right!

Once you see your design-driven products and services as portals to experiences that matter to your customers and grasp the need for experience supply chain management and are ready to walk the walk, you will take a look in the next chapter about how to talk the talk by learning a little about design language and how it becomes part of your strategy and how you build your product brand.

Your Products and Services Are Talking to People

How to make sure that they're saying the right thing—What is a design language?—Why is it important?—Thinking strategically.

You decide the primary family auto has been a good and faithful servant but it will soon be hitting its high-maintenance years, so you drive out to your city's motor mile, and wrestle your car's way through Saturday afternoon shopping traffic to where a string of various dealerships line the road. You start down the access road and glance into the lots, unaware that each suite of products is having a conversation with you, each brand making a design promise. What you are experiencing is design communication, a.k.a. as design language, and the most successful suites of product lines all have the touch of a designer behind them, one who consciously has orchestrated what you hear, see, and feel into a specific emotional response.

   This idea is an important part of your design strategy and should be considered and developed carefully. The "snick" of a door closing with firm

confidence, the sweep of the instruments on the dash, the position and shape of the gear shift, and every aspect of the exterior design—the latter being the first impression you get of a line of autos and how you can tell them most distinctly apart even if you saw them on the highway without their insignias.

You pause beside the Volvo dealership, and the vehicles are saying to you: safe, sturdy, well-built, and dependable. But really, some kind of look like they were evolved from metal shoeboxes struggling to be aerodynamically efficient. That might be fine for a soccer Mom and her kids getting to the school for an event, but you identify with sportier things, so you move on. Can't you have safety, dependability, quality workmanship like that, and yet have a car that handles well on a winding road and looks good when you're pulling up to the valet parking line of a quality restaurant?

The next dealership is BMW, and these cars are really talking to you. The model line looks as though they all share the same DNA. Your heart picks up a beat, and you turn in. You get out of your soon-to-be-retired auto and walk around a "Bimmer." It is different from each angle, but exciting with its long body and the sleek profile that combines for a sporty yet aggressive look. The distinctive kidney grill on the front you would know anywhere hints at a big engine that needs air. From the side, the car *looks* fast, thanks to the convex and concave synergy that the form creates. You don't know any of this, just have the sensations and emotions you experience. The roof line sweeps back in a gradual taper that stretches your sense of proportion of the whole car. From the back, you see the form from function contour aerodynamic design meant to optimize the flow of air. Both front and back seem low slung, even athletic, and the front overhang is short with large wheel arches as the car tapers back slightly wider powerful rear flanks. It looks like a dark cat poised to chew up the road.

You open the door and settle into the cockpit. At least it feels like that; the separation of seats by a center console and gear shifter along with the layout of the surrounding dash translate into an experience that promises to "fly" you down the road. Instead of one large flat dash and simple separations, the interior is marked by constant change, contrasting colors and textures, yet a unity of overriding design that is palpable in a sense of layering, with the center console sweeping to the rear seat and all of the beauty saying at the same time everything is where it is for a function, for a heightened experience no matter where you are in the car.

You climb out, shake off minor goose bumps, and decide that to be fair you need to see a few more of the car lots. You climb back into your auto, which is starting to look and feel a lot older and clumsier than it did when you set out, and you head for the next dealership, which happens to be the Hyundai lot. What's going on here? A lot of the cars look familiar, and this design language concept with which you are only beginning to feel familiar is, telling you a whole lot of mixed messages. It's like the Tower of Babel. That model looks kind of like it's pretending to be a BMW, and the one over there is almost an Acura. Another looks a bit like a Mercury, another

Toyota-ish, another with shades of Lexus, and so on. You get the same sensation at the Kia lot, and you even decide further along Auto Row, that Toyota got some of its sizzle from the designs of the German cars.

So you start thinking about which companies have product lines with design integrity, authority, and self-confidence showing through every aspect of their design, and now you are beginning to understand about design communication and why it matters.

The thing that is hard for most business people to grasp is that the design is there to tell a story. It takes a customer's need or desire and spins its story all the way to an expected fulfillment.

It's about a story—you see, the thing that is hard for most business people to grasp, is that the design language is there to tell a story. It takes a customer's need or desire and spins its story all the way to an expected fulfillment. Any writing class will tell you too that it is always better to "show" instead of just "tell." That's the exact function of design language. It shows. For that shopper at the BMW lot, the scenario playing through the mind might involve a drive up a winding Pennsylvania road in late spring, cornering the switchbacks with tight accuracy while the sound system fills the slick cockpit interior, finally pulling up to a country inn for brunch and being recognized as one of the "Bimmer" elite by fellow patrons.

Yet to another customer, who pulled into the Volvo dealership, the scenario playing is about driving in confident safety through an increasingly maddened morning rush to get the kids off to school, drop off Fluffy (the family cocker spaniel) at the vet for a grooming and checkup, and then head for the grocery store where the car's extra trunk space (even better with a station wagon) makes loading and unloading a breeze.

Different dreams, different answers, different design language, because design language also "defines" a product to its customer base.

It's about strategy—you can see this with any product or service. Take a house. A home buyer looks at each listing and makes each visit with a dream or expectation. Finally, the buyer sees one and says, "Oh, yeah. This is it. I can see us living here. I can see us entertaining, the kids having room to play, and it's got wonderful closet and storage space and the kitchen will be a dream to work in and there's workshop space." Its modern style fits your self image, and all the materials and details they use make you feel comfortable. You'd be proud to live in this house. The design language for the house is speaking. The house connected with you. You are the customer the designer intended to reach, and he was successful. For electronic products, and most products for that matter, where scale has to step in and thousands of people need to buy the product, the design communication has to be even more consistent about sharing its story, which is why it is so vital that the CEO and everyone else "get" how design language functions, and communicate clearly about it as they establish strategy for a product.

Take Dell's release of a new rugged model laptop in 2008, the Dell Latitude XFR D630. While the advertising does the telling, picking one up and looking at it lets the design language speak. It says, "Hey, my kids could haul this around in the backpacks to school where it could take a bump or bounce during the course of everyday use." Or, a business person could say, "The thing is not a beauty, but look at those rounded corners, built-in handle, its thick, heavier feel. This is a road warrior. Even though it's a bit more, we can save IT time if every sales rep is carrying one of these." The target audience is getting the story of the design language. One techno reviewer, though, clearly missed or misspoke the story and tried to compare and contrast the rugged Dell with Apple's MacBook Air.[29] The bloggers ate the reviewer alive, and when they did they made it clear they understood the design language of each disparate product. You take the Dell machine, designed to meet Pentagon durability standards and fit in a PC-business environment, and compare it one of the thinnest, sleekest Apple personal-use products, and you have a language mismatch.

All products communicate with customers. But you don't have to look hard to see many do that poorly, or spin the wrong story, or make promises that can't be kept.

You can be certain that neither Dell nor Apple misunderstood what the design communication of the two quite different products were supposed to accomplish, or what story they had been designed to share. This is why it is so important that an implicit understanding of how a design communication is part of the strategy of a suite of products must be understood by and employed by everyone in managing the customer experience supply chain. Once again; all products communicate with customers. But you don't have to look hard to see many that do so poorly, or spin the wrong story, or make promises that can't be kept. You need to be "spot on" with your design language story. The "how-to" part of making that happen is going to depend on you.

There are many things you need to do, from hiring good designers, changing how your development process works, making sure everyone contributing to the customer experience

understands their role and contribution, changing how you manufacture to support good design,
and so on, and so on. But one of the most important things you need to do is learn how to create
and implement design strategy. This will be the
cornerstone of everything. First, let's take a
closer look at design language to understand how
it leads to strategy.

And a critical piece of this is how the design
of your customer experience communicates to
people. In the "trades," we refer to this idea as a
design language.

What Is Design Language?

As a place to build from, let's start by taking a
look at Webster's definition for language:

lan·guage
Pronunciation: 'la[ng]-gwij, -wij

1 **a**: the words, their pronunciation, and the
methods of combining them used and
understood by a community **b** (1): audible,
articulate, meaningful sound as produced
by the action of the vocal organs (2): a
systematic means of communicating ideas
or feelings by the use of conventionalized
signs, sounds, gestures, or marks having
understood meanings (3): the suggestion by
objects, actions, or conditions of associated
ideas or feelings.

In reality, we use the idea of language as a
metaphor, which is not much of a stretch if we contemplate (2) and (3) above. Every time you see a

suite of products where the function and form have merged to say a distinctive and positive thing to you that evokes an emotional response in you, you are experiencing design language. It is the consciously orchestrated work of a designer, whether it is Michael Graves designing one of his colorful, yet whimsical, tea kettles with its distinctive egg motif, as sold at Target, or Sam Farber designing the puffy black handles of the affordable Good Grip kitchen utensils sold almost everywhere that make the kitchen a joy instead of a pain for those who suffer from arthritis.

If you make anything, you are saying things to people. If you make more than one thing, you are saying even more.

From the designer's point of view, if you make anything, you are saying things to people. If you make more than one thing, you are saying even more things. A Dutch designer named Adrian Van Hooydonk, for instance, is credited with a large part of the design language we have been talking about speaking to you when you were looking at the BMW and feeling a strong emotion without necessarily knowing why. In 2001, he was, though still in his 30s, design director in BMW's California car studio and design consultancy, Designworks, and he came up with the 7 series. Although the new 7 series was not universally loved at first site by the global Bimmer community, largely in reaction to the high rise truck lid, these design cues have since turned up all over the car-making world, including at Mercedes, Lexus, and Toyota. By 2004, Adrian took over design responsibility for all BMW designs under group design chief Chris Bangle, and his first task was to look to the design language, because, as he explained, "We changed our design language only because we needed to expand. Soon we'll have 10 car lines.

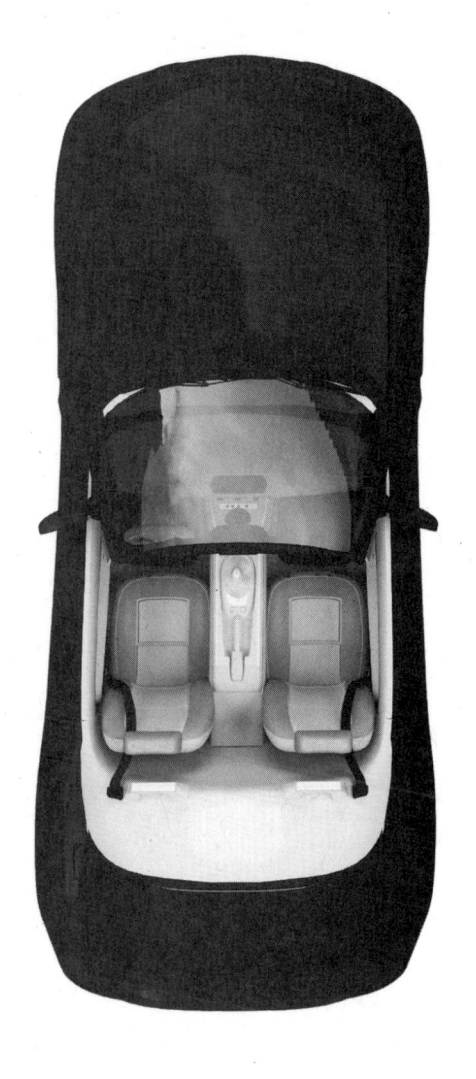

We had a successful design language, but it couldn't have stretched to 10 lines. We wanted to start the change while we were still successful. That's very BMW. If you wait until you're failing, the change will be scarier, more radical. Our goal wasn't to be radical."[30]

BWM needed to change its design language to expand its product line. So they started the change while they were successful, rather that waiting until the language was failing.

Following the idea that you can't please everyone and that it's best not to try, Adrian and his crew aimed to target the people attracted to owning "a driver's car," yet beauty needed to have the right mix with performance and function because while buying a car is an emotional experience, it also has to have a rational side. "Our goal is to communicate—through proportions, surfaces, stance—the performance, agility, and power."[31] That also involves integrity so that a car shouldn't look like it can corner well if it can't. Every factor has to be honest, bold, and come together for that tingle that goes up your spine.

Your products communicate with your consumers through design language. It is a compilation of forms, surfaces, materials, textures, graphics and colors, details and behavior, that all signal values. It is also how your product functions, what it does, and how it does it. It is its tone and tenor, and how it operates and sounds. Think of that iPod, iPhone, or sleek MacBook Air you just bought. What does it say when you see it, hold it, turn it on, and use it. Its design language is talking to you, and if you are Apple, believe me, this language is well thought out. Developing a design language program takes time and money. Doing so has obvious benefits.

Keep in mind that whereas almost every suite of products or services embodies a design language, they don't all work well. In many cases, that reflects tension between management and design. The customers don't know anything about what goes on behind the scenes, nor should they. However, they do sense what is being communicated to them, and if that message is totally garbled, they won't even consider the product or service. When you grasp the significance of design language, you'll begin to see many companies that get it wrong. But to reinforce our point, let's take a look at a company that gets it right, from one end to the other, with its customer experience supply chain management style.

When you walk into an IKEA store, you know you're not in your everyday furniture and fixture store. As we said with BMW, the function of design language is to define the audience, knowing that it's not for everyone. The BMW message is focused. It is all about performance, prestige, authenticity, and great German design and craftsmanship. But as with any great brand, the message is focused and a broader customer base is attracted by this focus because it is aspirational. People want to buy into it and be that focused individual that BMW is "targeting" with its design.

At IKEA, your experience is varied, and the mix is in large part the design language of every aspect of the company pointing you to where the real focus of the store is pointed—quality furniture at affordable prices. The parking lot wasn't much different from most, and so far the clerks are far from Nordstrom interactive. In fact, you weave through a pretty populated store and are left more to your own devices than not. But what does catch your eye are the clean lines and solid clear quality of the products. You also notice

Whereas almost every suite of products made embodies a design language, they all do not work well, In many cases, that reflects tension between management and design.

At IKEA, your experience is varied, and the mix is in large part the design language of every aspect of the company pointing you to where the real focus of the store is—quality, well-designed furniture at affordable prices.

how they are fitting their products into your life. How they are helping you make good choices. And how this modern lifestyle makes you feel cool, hip, and smart. And the prices are good. Real good. But you get the feeling everything is going to come in a box and you're going to have to assemble it. The displays are great, whole rooms as they would function, and let you see how each object could function in your home, there's a product trial period, and there's also a canteen where you can take a break.

You decide on an entertainment center and there's a hiccup or two before you have the box on a cart. When you check out, there's a line, and you end up with a box in the car when what you would really like is someone to deliver the darn thing and assemble it. But you did get one heck of a good price on something that's going to last and will make your house look great.

You get home and prepare for one of those "some assembly required" experiences that can make the night before Christmas a nightmare, but you become pleasantly surprised. Instead of one of those fine-print jumbles in a dozen languages other than yours, you get clear step-by-step illustrations with a Ziggy-sort of cartoon style that every person putting together the object together at home can understand because it speaks in emotions. You see the cartoon character was unhappy when the corner of a cabinet broke, so you put a rug under your assembly area. You relate to the character's joys and frustrations, and before you know it, you have your new unit together and it looks great. When its products are displayed and shipped around the world (in nearly forty editions to almost thirty countries in more than a dozen languages), what better way to avoid awkward repetitions and achieve clear, simple assembly than by using the language of emotion. This is all part of the design language that targets and connects with the general masses of upwardly mobile nest builders everywhere who seek good design, modern lifestyle, and quality at a fair price. They are communicating this to you through the store, the banners, the layout, and of course, the products. Everything. It is all about how design communicates to you, and that you get the message loud and clear.

Speaking in Tongues

Realizing that design language to a large degree engages emotionally with the intended customer (or prospective customer) base rather than primarily through logic, you can see why most managers have trouble embracing the importance of this idea. It's a concept for them that's hard to wrap their heads around. Part of the resistance might come from fear of giving up control in a design driven environment. But if this is all approached in the way we've been suggesting—as customer experience supply chain management—the upper managers of any company will have just as much participation in how things are done, and they'll also be part of the unfolding success story.

While the head of design does not need to be the tail that wags the dog, in a design-driven company, design does permeate everything. At Apple, even the company announcements that go up on the wall move through the design department to ensure the company maintains a unified language that shows in every product and service. Unfortunately, when most companies decide to define and create their design language, they do it for many well-intentioned reasons that ultimately take them off target.

In our experience, clients who ask for a design language of their own cite the need for differentiation and consistency, and want to save money by leverage of time, resources, and materials. All good reasons.

Interestingly enough, very few cite communication to customers or brand definition or relationship with end users as reasons to invest in language projects. What is wrong with this way of thinking is:

- Consistency is not always the right answer. Many of your products do need to differ from one another. But this should be on purpose, not by accident.

- Thinking only about competitors takes the spotlight off you. You need to carve out your competitive position, but core language values should be more permanent. More about you. Markets and trends change quickly. You should adapt to this, but hang on to your core values.

- Leverage is a good thing operationally, but can create compromise. It does not matter if you saved time or money this way, if nobody wants the stuff you are selling. Be careful with leverage. It always sounds good on paper. In the end, it should be about great ideas and great products and services. Saving a few bucks or a little time inappropriately could kill this.

The most often overlooked reason to think about design language is that your products are speaking to people—telling them things about what it does, how it does it, and what your company is about. It is connecting with them and also telling them things about themselves. Not with everybody, but with certain people. It makes sense to think about who and how, doing all you can to connect with them in a powerful way.

The role of design here needs to go far beyond simply devising forms or details, or the selection of three-dimensional motifs to differentiate a company's desired market position. Rather, design should create products and services that dramatize the company's core values in the form of concrete customer experiences and emotional responses.

One more time—this is not exactly an easy thing to do.

The role of design here needs to go far beyond simply devising forms or details to differentiate a company's desired market position. Rather, design should create products and services that dramatize the company's core values.

Getting to Your Own Design Language and Strategy

Creating language is a process, not an event. Business is a process, not an entity. Successful businesses constantly adapt to change. They behave more like organisms than organizations. Creating a good design strategy needs to recognize this. Old school thinking is about creating rules and boundaries, thus creating design systems that prized uniformity and consistency to a fault. Problem is, in today's world, they are out of date before the ink dries, and the reality is that one size does not fit all. What we need are new design language systems that sacrifice those rigid qualities in favor of being alive and dynamic.

This is something you need to build into all of what you do. It's not just a one-time thing. It's a "real time," always present aspect of how you manage what your products or services are saying. Design language as it is alive and used today is attuned to our more conversational markets and to those willing and eager to articulate their needs, wants, and dreams as well as voice dissatisfaction when those are not met. It tells a story that unfolds over time. It creates relationships through discovery and satisfaction.

Design is not a statement, but a dialog. It is a story that needs to be written in a cohesive and flowing way.

Design is not a statement, but an ongoing dialog. You need to understand the story your customers want to hear, and that has to be written in a cohesive and flowing way, not assembled from something like rough blocks you jam together. Think again of the word *orchestrate*. All this has to come together as part of one strategic plan that is based on customer emotion.

How you go about creating and developing a design language specific to your product lines or service lines depends on what you want to say to your target consumers. The message should be consistent, recognizable, and rest on an emotional foundation.

Begin with building on who you are. However well you think you know what you are up to, you need to experience a refreshed self-awareness, a "know thyself," as Socrates would say. You need to explore and build a deeper understanding of your brand and product experience. To figure out your brand, let's go back to the Marty Neumeier questions we posed in Chapter 3, "How To Matter":

- Who are you?

- What do you do?

- Why does it matter?

We asserted earlier that most companies have no difficulty with the first, some trouble with the second, and have no clue about the third. For instance, are you in the automobile business, or are you in the business of making reliable, affordable transportation ideal to a selected consumer base? If you went away, would customer's shrug and slip effortlessly to a competitor, or would they clamor as loudly as the thousands upon thousands who had a huge collective "hissy fit" when Coke went to New Coke. Or worse, could your business go the way of the Dodo and Polaroid and Sharper Image. Getting this clear and candid picture is why it might be best to hire professionals to help you. Like people, companies are prone to flatter themselves and not be as brutally honest with themselves as they should be. Outsiders are best in this case because they can be objective and really see you for who you are, not who you *think* you are.

Characterize what makes your company vital. Understand if and why you matter. Define your attributes. You should build a manageable set of words that describe who you are and what you offer. Then look at the basic qualities you communicate and the ideas that make up your products, and the values that people should perceive. Use what you discover about yourself as a dialog with people, both inside and outside, to reach agreement on what your products are really about. What you learn should become part of your goals and a means of measurement. Long ago, L.L. Bean and Abercrombie & Fitch had to wake up and say, "Hey, we're not really sporting goods companies anymore. Most of our sales are coming from clothing, shoes, and accessories to puppy yuppies. We need to retool for that." And they did.

Own the idea of who you are. Dedicate resources to building it. This might mean bringing in a design consultant, hiring design staff, or converting your whole company, the way Samsung did. Have a constant dialogue within your organization to continually refine and hone your approach. Hear and listen to what your constituents think, but don't simply react to what they say. Don't spend too much time looking at the competition. Like your brand, your identity is a living organism in the guts of your customers, like those Harley Davidson faithfuls.

You need to not only just listen to what your customers say but interpret what they are expressing, and from that make inferences about what they think. Instead of focus groups and traditional research, you need to watch what people do, observe what they use, as well as how they see, feel, hear, touch, and interact with every aspect of a product. You need to experience epiphanies about what they know and really understand how they feel, even if they don't express or communicate that as clearly as you would like, and from that you need to appreciate their dreams—what they really want or need. When you grasp that, you might find you need to change the way you do things.

You can only do that if you can get to a company-wide commitment, with strong leadership up and down the ranks, and especially an absolute buy-in at the top, because a partial change, or minor adjustment, or a tweak here and there is the kind of band-aid on a balloon that marked the demise of companies that thought they mattered, but found they didn't. You need to incorporate a design strategy that acts as an overriding tool that you use across the management experience supply chain to help guide these customer experience-driven developments of all you extend to your targeted consumer base.

Build it in. You need to ensure that the revised sense of customer experience you gain is built into the language of who you are, what you do, and why that matters. You must work to create product design that supports the brand attributes and works to further the proposition. Look at your line and prioritize the attributes for each offering. You should land on a unified approach that extends through different elements, both physical and operational. This means focusing on product behaviors as much as visuals. Look not only at how things look, but how things sound, how they operate, how things work. You should define your ideal brand experience. What do you want people to feel when they come in contact with your company? Build the kind of scenarios they should experience, write stories your design language should be sharing. This should lead to the building of the perfect emotional framework for your company and brand that allows you to use words and ideals that can be defined tangibly to create an ideal vision.

Focus on product behaviors as much as visuals. Look not only at how things look, but how things sound, how they operate, and how they work.

From that you build a prototype experience in the purest form of what you want your customer to see. These will be real things—models, boxes, displays, stores, and so on, but also shares your ideals, your philosophy, and your boundary conditions for your experience. Then you test it. Not for popularity, but to see what people really think. How does it make them feel? What do they get from it? What turns them on, or, more importantly, off. Refine all that, then go out and build it into your process.

If great design resided in research alone, there would be more great design.

All of what you do should support and be consistent to the brand. Customer experience should be part of the brand that identifies and defines your products. Think too of aiming toward achieving icons and avatars (as used in a derivative design sense for a product—spin-off products that clearly fit with the suite or line).

Creating an iconic product can provide a halo effect over your entire product line that will lift the equity of all your products. It can serve to redefine who you are and set your language in an entirely new direction. The trick is figuring out how to leverage the icon in a meaningful way (see the Razr story in Chapter 1, "Design Matters"). A single product that is an exceptional portal to a spectrum of experiences that matter to customers can make or remake an entire company, as is the case with the iPod. It is important to take these opportunities to present your language in its purest, most iconic form.

You need to observe trends, but ignore them when it comes to your brand. There is danger in surfing trends. When it's over, you are screwed. It's best to be yourself and look at trends as context. You need to keep your products flexible and scalable. It is bad business when a language hurts a single product for the "good of the whole." A good design language is not about a singular design scaled to fit whatever product you want to ship. This can truly damage a product where your existing language simply won't scale. Rather, a good language is an ethos and an idea, with a well-defined vocabulary to make things fit together. You construct your design statements using this vocabulary. You don't jam a successful idea from the past and force-fit it into your future. Rather, like BMW, you evolve your design language to inform expanding lines.

A design language is by no means "marching orders," but should bend enough to allow every product to be its best. You need to manage all this continually. This is not a science. It needs discussion, ongoing development, constant care, and awareness, which is why it might be best to seek professional design help. Again, language is a process not an event. This will build over time. Stay focused on this. Continue to have dialogs and build a shared understanding. This is how your language will develop.

In the next chapter, it's "all together now" as we bring all the elements together so you can consider what it will take for you to make the "leap of faith" into becoming a more design-driven company.

Building a Design-Driven Culture

You have to design and build the organizational culture to serve the intended customer experience. If you don't do this, you cannot achieve success that lasts.

Throughout this book, you have seen many examples of companies that get it right, and others that don't. Here's the thing. It's possible that five years from now some might have slipped, while others might have found their stride again. It has become something of a spectator sport for people to look at the companies offered as models in books like *In Search of Excellence*, *Built to Last*, or *Good to Great* to see how they've done lately, particularly if they appear to have faltered or lost their way a bit. We believe there are lessons for us all if we look to learn rather than to be right. Ideas are important. Start with the ideas and the specifics of the "how to" will be forthcoming. What follows are a few broad brushstrokes.

Life and business are all about change, and that calls for an approach that centers on a culture built to deal with change. A design-driven company has that. Who is to say that Apple, IKEA, BMW, and others might not stumble. But it's less likely if they stay true to the course they are on. So, we're not giving you models to watch and copy, but examples of what works or

doesn't work so you can understand the design-driven approach and use it yourself. We've drawn examples from an array of products and services to help you begin thinking in a generalized way about how design affects every aspect of almost everything. It is up to you to put the ideas to work so as to ensure that the ultimate all-around experience of your customer is something special. We have witnessed too many corporate meetings where concern for the customer experience is not even a concept, let alone a driver of design. A design-driven corporate culture is also not a "plug it in and there you go" kind of package. The basics are adaptable to different circumstances and environments.

Let's look at some of the core aspects of a design-driven company. They represent a consolidation of ideas we have explored so far. It just so happens that they can be arranged to form the acronym FLAVOR. A lot of business books seem determined to add yet another acronym to the heaping pile and purport that it will be the Holy Grail or panacea for the ills of business. Well, we aren't trying to do that—we just couldn't help ourselves. In fact, it would be better if you just think of FLAVOR as a mnemonic for easily recalling some of the core aspects as you create a design for customer experience supply chain management. Here is what the letters stand for:

- Focus
- Long-term
- Authentic
- Vigilant
- Original
- Repeatable

Now, let's zoom in and explore what each one means, and how they must synchronize and work together.

Focus

You go to check in at a La Quinta Inn at 11 a.m. and ask if you can check in early so you can wind down from travel, clean up, and be ready for a 3:30 p.m. meeting. Sarah, the reception clerk says, "Sorry. We can't let anyone check in before 3 p.m. so the maids have time to clean all the rooms." You try to get the clerk to bend, but it's not possible, she says. You think, "This isn't about what is convenient for me. It's about what's convenient for them." So you cancel your reservation, drive to the Sheraton, and they let you in right away. Somewhere up the experience chain at La Quinta someone has made a rigid rule that no one checks in before 3 p.m. Or, and this is more likely, that's just the way the clerk hears or perceives this is the way things work and doesn't feel empowered enough to buck it. In time, the rigidity is part of the experience and the CEO begins to scratch a bewildered head and wonders why the numbers are slipping.

Contrast this with the Nordstrom clerk, or the one at Whole Foods who goes into the back room to get you exactly what you want. Huge difference. A measurable difference. A "Do You Matter" difference. A difference of focus. A focus on the customer experience. This is the emphasis on clearly architecting what you put out that people see, touch, and feel, and how it defines you in their hearts.

The focus should always be on the customer experience. Your entire organizational culture must be aligned to deliver on this idea.

Your entire organizational culture—in other words, how everybody thinks, behaves, and is rewarded—must be aligned to deliver on the design of the intended customer experience. This is customer experience supply chain management at work.

This focus on what your customers feel is not just for front-line employees. It's key to every aspect of a service or product. Focus on not just the design of the experience and then on the delivery, focus also on the customers' emotional response to that delivery. Look to see if they respond in the way you intended. Notice if they discover desirable qualities about your products and services that represent serendipitous outcomes of the development process rather than something that was consciously designed in at the beginning. What your customer values might come as a surprise to you, or at least not be fully understood. This is a really big idea. It is so easy to imagine they will value what you value. They value what they value. Maybe that matches what you value. Maybe not.

Polaroid is a really great example of a company not understanding the valued experience. Because, what was always so fantastic about Polaroid cameras was not the film, it was the instant gratification, the *instant*. Click, bzzzt, you watched the picture develop. That was the experience. It was simple. You point, you push the button; you get a picture. There was the whole magic quality of how it occurred, and the cameras had this interesting quality about them. If ever a company should have been the first to grasp the significance of digital photography, it should have been Polaroid. I mean, it was

Polaroid that *invented* the instant experience; that was the benefit. But through the years, they came to think it was about the camera. They worried about protecting their film business. The worst form of arrogance is thinking the customer's experience isn't your teacher. One of the saddest scenarios is where companies get this, then forget it or lose it or become unresponsive.

If the customer says, "Hey, can I get my name on my shoes? I'd be willing to pay more for that." Nike says, "Can do." If a person wants his or her picture on a bottle of soda, Jones Soda says, "Coming right up." If you want your company name on your business credit cards, the Advanta Bank Corporation says you can, and that helps it stand out in the crowd. If you're the business that's still standing with planted feet while saying, "No. It's not about what's convenient for you, or neat, or fun for you. It's about what's most convenient to us," then pretty soon you'll end up on life support or in an untimely grave.

But don't get us wrong. This is not about just saying yes all the time and always giving people what they want. That is not the right approach. It is about understanding their needs and desires, and meeting them. And doing it in a way uniquely yours that has them loving your company. This is ultimately what design will do for you.

This is not about just saying yes all the time. It is about understanding your customer's needs and desires, and meeting them.

Long-Term

Legend has it that shortly before his death, Mao Zedong was asked what he thought about the French Revolution. "Too soon to tell" was his answer. (Actually, it's a good guess that it was

Chou En Lai, an avid student of French history, who said this, though precisely when, or to whom, isn't clear.) While we are not proposing this concept of long-term here, we nevertheless want to make the point that this peculiarly American preoccupation with instant gratification is not a good trait when you want to realign your culture to the realities of becoming one that is design driven. It takes a deliberate practice and time.

It takes long-term deliberate focus on the customer experience supply chain to produce instant delight and gratification for your customers.

Samsung is a great example of how they've used design over the last 10 years to really redefine themselves as a world electronics leader. Every year they get incrementally better at what they're doing, to the point where they've pretty much eclipsed Sony. Samsung products are landing on the objects of lust lists put out by the media. Their equity in people's minds is really high. That was an overt strategy; it did not just happen. The thing is, they decided more than 10 years ago they were going to become a design leader. With a step-by-deliberately-design-driven-step process in place, Samsung is pulling it off.

At the risk of being a little tongue in cheek, we assert that it takes a long-term deliberate focus on the customer experience supply chain to produce instant gratification and delight for your customers. Apple seems to get this, as does IKEA, BMW, and Harley Davidson, along with the other businesses we have cited as being design driven. But, again, don't do like they do. Do like *you* need to do. Every business must design its own long-term strategy tailored to all the aspects that orchestrate delivery of what matters to its customer base, this year, and next year, and the years after that.

As Yves Béhar, designer of the Leaf Lamp and the $100 laptop, and founder of FuseProject, puts it, "Design is not a short-term fix. It's a long-term engagement that requires you to think about how design affects everything that touches the consumer—from product to packaging to marketing to retail to the take-home experience."[32]

All you really need to do to grasp this concept is look around and find the companies that you can identify as design driven and see who is still around. Who keeps reinventing themselves and who always seems fresh and unique in a world where things all too quickly become the same and evolve into yet another commodity. It is not enough to do this just once, to be a one-trick pony. You have to do it again and again and again, and to do that you have to have design throughout the fabric of your company and it has to be an active ingredient and it has to be part of your future quite a ways out.

Authentic

As recognized in the case of the airlines, the idea can be as sound as you like, but if the crew, for whatever reason, doesn't focus on creating great customer experiences, and instead allow the flight to be an aerial roller-coaster trip through hell, then all the other elements are wasted. If your slogan is "We Care," this had better be the case. If your customer is to have this experience, and if you are the CEO, you and your senior team had better practice behaviors that your employees experience are consistent with the slogan; that the company cares about them too. Otherwise, they will just be going through

The bottom line is that your customers are smarter and more perceptive than you think. It has to be real and based on a commitment. Or people will feel it.

the motions with your customers, wondering all the while what exactly are the motions they are supposed to be going through. Authenticity matters. Authenticity demands that corporate and individual behavior be consistent with the intended experience design. Bottom line is that your customers are smarter and more perceptive than you think. It has to be real and based on a commitment. Or people will feel it, and they will suspect they are being deceived. People are learning to be aware of empty words.

If we continue with the airlines as an example, you've got all the other carriers in there battling it out, and along comes Branson, and founds Virgin. His board thought it was a lousy idea and he did it anyway. The brand is aspirational (you see, the language thing again). An aspirational product, service, or brand, is one that a significant portion of the market desires but maybe can't afford, or it's one that shares its sizzle with the user who is aware that he or she is getting in on something that not everyone gets to enjoy. A lot of people, especially as you get to the younger generations, want to be a rock star, want to be treated like a rock star, be associated with something like that, so that's where the Virgin experience appeals.

They really have succeeded in building Virgin Airlines as an iconic brand in a very short amount of time. Now what did they do differently? And why could they do it. Why are United and American struggling to provide a great customer experience? (You can figure out the answers by now.) Will Virgin be able to maintain altitude as they grow? They've built a classic, narrowly focused brand and, to quote one of their ads: "We have more experience than our name would suggest." With Virgin America, they are trying to cross over to engage a broader customer base. The iPod was narrowly focused on the younger generation and successfully crossed over to become multi-generational. Can Virgin do this? Without Branson? Too soon to tell.

If Virgin America can take that sort of, "Hey-we're-a-little-hip," rock star idea, and build it out, they could be very successful. In the design strategy process, they have to ask, "How are they going to design the continuing experience?" They've got this core brand that's associated with edgy, rock, that sort of vibe, and want to take it mainstream and still continue to build that cache that'll make people want to join their parade. If you're a low-cost carrier, you can get away with a little funkiness and being a little different. But it can't be artificial funkiness. It has to be the real thing, and that makes all the difference. People can tell if it is not authentic. If it's all just a veneer, they'll flip the bozo bit on you like they did on Motorola.

A good example of design strategy that achieved and sustained authenticity was the IBM ThinkPad. As we speculated earlier, it's going to be interesting and perhaps sad to see what Lenovo does now that it has acquired the ThinkPad line. If the company doesn't "get" what makes the product matter to its customers, they are likely to destroy it. If you look at IBM when they started the ThinkPad line, they took some of the corporate feel of their products, and then Richard Sapper, who developed this very minimal, functional-looking, almost military grade product. And they

Virgin has built a classic, narrowly focused brand that is not only aspirational, but authentic.

© Michael F. McLaughlin

realized it struck a chord with business people, and they continued to develop that and refine it. It's very clearly a positioning strategy. When you look at all the notebooks in the world, the two iconic notebook brands were the ThinkPad and the PowerBook. And they're very different. IBM very overtly went about doing that, saying "We're going to be different from Apple."

If a business person interested in design had to buy a Windows-based notebook, nine out of ten times he or she tended to choose a ThinkPad. IBM is not necessarily a cool brand, but it is authentic, used very clearly as a continuing positioning strategy. With great success. Lenovo now needs to nurture the brand and leverage the equity that came with the brand.

Clearly, authenticity is also yours to lose. Recall what happened to Dell when in the name of saving money it outsourced customer service, and many middle Americans, whether from legitimate concerns or just down-home xenophobia, claimed it couldn't understand the customer service reps. This was almost like a tipping point in reverse—where a company does something that damages them. So Dell scrambled and went into damage control mode and perhaps spent all the money they thought they'd saved trying to make things right. The same thing happened when Home Depot tried to save money by switching to inexpensive labor instead of continuing with their foundational strategy, which was to employ retired contractors who really could deliver on the promise "you can do it, we can help." The loss of authenticity doesn't always come from money issues, but often it does, and the public can smell and sense deception along with broken promises.

It's so very easy to do; to destroy or cripple everything you've built. Some front-line manager makes a crazy decision and nobody catches it in time, and you can destroy your brand. JetBlue is a testimonial to this. The company was climbing the skies with a burgeoning business base on a unique, authentic experience, and then suddenly you leave people stranded for eleven hours on a runway and things start to slip. They didn't cause the initial hit; weather did. But in weeks, the crews weren't as chipper, the on-board snacks were suddenly downsized, and the authentic energy was fading. Along the way, their stock price has fallen to around $5.00 (as we write this), down from around $27.00 when they were flying high. In a just-released survey, JetBlue made the top three for customer satisfaction and is now gaining altitude again.

The loss of authenticity does not always come from money issues, but it often does, and the public can smell and sense deception along with broken promises.

Authenticity is again a system-wide thing. If Betty, at her checkout at Wal-Mart, draws more customers to her line, but her manager doesn't understand that what's going on is authenticity at work, then it's a random event that's largely wasted as far as impacting the corporate culture goes. Authenticity is missing in a product if something looks as if it will last forever but
the damn thing falls apart as soon as you get it home. And the authenticity really slips to the dark side when you try to get the broken thing fixed or replaced, and you get a customer service rep who you quickly perceive would just as soon take a long walk on a short pier. Authenticity is something you can't fake on any level. The consequences of getting caught trying to fake it can be terminal.

Vigilant

You need to constantly stay on top of the customer experience supply chain. Change is going to happen. That's a given. Some of your vigilance is going to be watching your competitors, but don't waste a lot of cycles thinking that's where the enemy is. The enemy is you if you pull a Polaroid and get beaten at the game you invented. You need to be relentless to get great design out to the market. You need to sweat the details. By way of example, Apple designers spend 10 percent of their time on concept, and 90 percent on implementation.

Design-driven vigilance is a considered awareness. It's not stark paranoia that makes you determine your strategy based on what the competition is doing. The folks at BlackBerry are obviously aware of the iPhone. If they are being true to their own culture, they are also looking to the future and a design strategy that will keep their brand alive and vigorous in the guts of their customers. As we write this, BlackBerry devices have about 40 percent of the Smart phone business, while the iPhone has garnered about 25 percent (in a little more than six months). Apple is now deploying their exceptional abilities to make the iPhone enterprise friendly and have added push email, an official Software Developers Kit, and a brilliant distribution model for native iPhone applications. Apple is poised to be the dominant player in the smart phone space for the next decade or two.

We know we are beating the Apple example to death, but it drives home the point. The goal was to make a mobile phone device people loved. The iPhone is a great user experience. End of story. Apple's approach to design—a vigilant focus on what mattered to the end user—drove development and shaped all the technology to pull off a marvel of convergence. Apple changed the game. Now everybody is eating their dust. Research In Motion (RIM), the developers of BlackBerry, will be under tremendous pressure. They definitely need to matter to their current customers. And they have to continue to lead with design in a way that is both authentic and relentless. They cannot start to chase.

Vigilance is also "forward looking" as well as keeping track of what is going on around you. In that way, it's like continuous due diligence. You want to prospect and prognosticate about future trends as they are shaping. Will manufacturing continue its shift to the Pacific Rim, or will factions continue to expand in Brazil, Mexico, or elsewhere? On a recent trip to China, we met a leading footwear designer who was making the journey to begin moving some manufacturing lines to North Vietnam because it was cheaper. As a global society, will we get the underlying message of the MasterCard Priceless campaign, that "there are some things in life money can't buy, for everything else...?" At the end of the day, it is about the experience. A relentless focus on price and cost structures can easily degrade the customer experience to the point that no one cares about you anymore.

People will pay a premium for a better experience. In fact this might be the *only* thing that they will consistently pay a premium for. That's a hard concept for the Excel crowd to get.

But more than anything else, vigilance is about working great design across the system.

Vigilance is also "forward looking" as well as keeping track of what is going on around you. In a way, it's like continuous due diligence.

More than anything else, vigilance is about working great design across the system. If you take your eyes off the ball, it will degrade. This is just human nature.

If you take your eyes off the ball, it will degrade. This is just human nature. The natural forces of entropy. To do great design, you must be willing to invest all the way across the customer experience supply chain. In the case of a product, it is not just the concept, but also every detail until it gets into your customers' hands. And then some.

Original

You might think originality is just about being different, off the wall, outside the box. That's one perception, but this is really the area where the approach to risk matters, and the approach to research matters. Research can actually hold back originality, especially when it comes to the committee style of thinking to be found in traditional focus groups. How valuable research is to the design effort and to understanding the customer experience depends on who does it. Some people do it very well and some people don't, and some people don't do it at all. Apple does very little research.

Research is a tool to be used diligently and appropriately. It's not the end-all. A lot of times, if used improperly, it can actually lead to bad design, or even worse, mediocre design. The goal of research should not be to purely sample public opinion. The goal of the research, relative to design, is to discover an opportunity, design to the opportunity, and then validate what you've come up with to see if you got it right. Of course, there are a variety of forms of research, and different ways of understanding demographics and getting to know what it is that a certain sector of people like and don't like. As you're developing products, it's important to understand all this stuff, who you are trying to target, as well as the experience you want to provide. That's really important. Where research becomes a trap is when it crosses over to risk mitigation. The old "we'll go out and sample some small groups of people and see what they think of our design" trap.

The challenge is that really good innovative design tends to break norms, and most people right off the street have a hard time getting their heads around that. They like what they know. They like things that are familiar, maybe a little beyond familiar, but not much. You present something new to people like that and most won't vote for something that's too original. They might if they come to use it for awhile. But they can't articulate an experience they haven't had yet. People have a hard time getting outside their normal idea of what a product is and can do. We've observed an example recently that was developed in a careful and extensive manner to create a fantastic new experience. However, upon the release, the product was jumped upon by the media and blogs. In these cases, the vast majority of the negative review was from people who had never actually seen the device "in the flesh," let alone used one. But those "early adopters" who had experienced using the product, loved it. The main lesson here is that although people's initial reaction was often negative, as word of mouth from deliriously happy users has grown, the device has become recognized as the best in its category ever created. And the manufacturer cannot build them fast enough.

So the key to using research effectively is to identify your target customer, to observe their lives, to discover the things that are giving

Design research should not be a popularity contest, as many people cannot always relate to or fully understand new ideas.

them trouble, discover the things that are giving them pleasure, all that emotional-level content, and then use that information to go off and develop ideas.

At some point, later on, when you think you've got something, you set it down in front of the same people and see if they can turn it on, see if they can find the power button or not. You also want to learn how people feel about it, which is not the same as whether they like it. If you go for that before the idea has been fleshed out into a design-driven product, you might see good ideas get shot down or watered down just to try and build some consensus among a diverse group of people. When it comes to building a successful brand, you need to be about focus, so you don't want to try and make everybody happy. You want to find something that certainly doesn't offend a lot of people, and most of all, you want to excite people and draw them in, have them feel as if they are joining something. We like to employ the 80/20 rule. You want 80 percent of the market to love it. But also you'd like 20 percent to be challenged by it.

We like to employ the 80/20 rule. You want 80 percent of the market to love it. But you'd also like 20 percent to be challenged by it.

Risk is a necessary part of being original. At Apple, it is part of the deliberate strategy, and has been so for so long that it's now almost cultural DNA. Failing is fine if you are trying to move the bar forward. If you are just stupid and fail, then you are likely to be labeled an idiot and you don't last. On the other hand, for people who are trying to do something new with an idea aimed at moving forward, their attempt is celebrated even if the product doesn't sell. One of the Apple marketing talents presented that the second or third generation of any product always outsold the first generation by a mile. The first generation would be an inch tall on a bar graph, and the next one would be three inches, and the next one would be six inches, because of the learning that occurred.

In design, risk is not a four-letter word. You have to take chances to get anywhere.

Apple constantly learned about what was good and what was not, so the customer base kept building, accepting that the product would improve and anticipating that change. With the realization that this was the natural course of things, the strategy at Apple included the notion that you shouldn't give up just because an idea didn't sell 15 million units of the first generation implementation. If it sold 100,000 and you found out what was good and what was not, and you could see the potential, then keep going.

When you seek to balance risk and research on the path to originality, it's no easy feat. Many companies employ a management technique where with every project, they set up the boundary conditions, usually around cost and schedule, and there will also be technology conditions. But there is a problem if the development teams see these as hard boundaries. At Apple, we used to say to the team "it's all right to play in this field; if you cross one of these boundaries, a red flag goes up and we just need to review it and understand it." This didn't mean you couldn't cross a boundary. You just need to know when you *have* crossed one.

More than risk mitigation, you need a program for risk support. If you are going to be design driven to create original products and services, your favorite new mantra needs to be: "Risk is not a four-letter word."

Think risk support rather than mitigation. You have to ask "What are the boundary conditions around that design that are going to break it if we keep trying to pull things out?" The risk here is you take the soul out of product. It takes a soft skill set, more of an art than a science, a sort of "just knowing" what it is that's making that products great and where those boundaries are. And, of course, that's what makes most left-brain business people more than a little nervous.

You need to allow the design people the freedom, at least initially, to explore nudging the boundaries and use design and the creative mind to do that. A general rule, when managing creative talent, is it's a lot easier to rein people in than to get them to expand and run free as time goes on. Visualize the process as a funnel. You're constantly narrowing down toward a solution. It should always be very wide open to possibilities at the beginning, and as you get further along, it is time to be very tight and focused. You keep it sort of broad and open at first, then narrow it down. As a business person, you are building a design-driven culture that's organized around providing a superior experience to the end user. This means that your creative talent is managed within that context. There'll also be testing; but that will always be in the same context: that of the customer experience and how they engage emotionally with your product or service.

The creative process is really hard to compress; it really is very difficult. You just need time to experiment and try things. Because when you get compressed, what you do is you revert to what you know.

A really important part of a design-driven culture is that you give people the ability to experiment. Failure can be OK, as long as you are trying to move things forward.

One of the real challenges you have right now, that's been growing in America and around the world, is time compression. If you've got a week to create something, you're probably going to follow the things you know and can do and execute very well, as opposed to exploring breakthroughs if given the time and space. Now, the challenge in today's global economy where time to market is a necessary obsession, is how do you allocate time and space? If there's a market opportunity that needs to be fulfilled in nine months, and it takes eight months to engineer and tool something, then basically you're giving your design team a month. And that happens more times than not. What to do?

You make haste slowly. You must allow time for research and development to happen in the design space. You have to. Even if it's not part of the mainstream day-to-day "get it out in nine months project," you can move it outside and say here's another project, this is a study, this is another ongoing long-term thing, and you're going to give people the ability to spend time exploring, to do trial and error. It's a really important quality of a design-driven culture, that as part of a project or on a parallel path, you give people the ability to experiment, to practice trial and error and have a few failures and learn from them and move on. Otherwise, you won't move the bar ahead, you'll just get stuck in the same rut.

Repeatable

In science, when you complete an experiment, nothing is proven until you can show that the results are repeatable. In business, that doesn't mean imitating yourself. And in respect to being design driven, it takes on an even more charged and dynamic meaning: It means being able to do the same thing again, only differently.

Back to the iPhone again. The story is particularly remarkable when you consider how in six months it became the number-two smart phone (after the BlackBerry). Apple did this with a first-generation product. They didn't use the same design path as the iPod, but they used the same creative approach, which is to focus on the customer experience and make a device people love. You ask how would you design this if the BlackBerry didn't exist? As the product establishes its own market, it will continue to evolve, like the iPod, only different because the phone market is a different arena. Both benefited from the Apple culture. When you have built a design-driven culture, the design process can happen more rapidly. In a world where time to market is a make or break deal, not having a design-driven culture is a fatal flaw in this respect alone.

Many companies have come and gone. The reason for the departure of many was an inability to keep reinventing themselves. The concept applies in almost every category, and to further illustrate everything we've just talked about, why don't we look at one more company that clearly "got it;" that is design driven from one end to the other.

If you've ever been in the kitchen section of any general merchandise store or specialty stores like Williams Sonoma, you have seen knives, peelers, can-openers, tea kettles, and any of a number of products with chubby soft black grips. The spongy handles also have flexible soft fins on the sides. These are Good Grip products and they are the brain child of OXO International, a company that began with a design idea.

Sam Farber's wife Betsey was an architect who had arthritis in her hands so bad that being in the kitchen was no longer the joy it once was; it had become a difficult and frustrating experience. Sam had retired from being CEO of Copco, a cookware company he had founded in 1960 that was known for cookware products of colorful enameled cast iron with teak handles. The couple had rented a house in the South of France to focus on fun: cooking, entertaining, and their love of art. But when Sam saw Betsey struggling with culinary tools in the kitchen, he put his designer cap back on.

To Sam, it made no sense that anyone should have to suffer while doing the things that fulfill their passions. Why hadn't anyone come up with an answer before for the 20 million Americans

The reason for the departure of many companies was an inability to keep reinventing themselves.

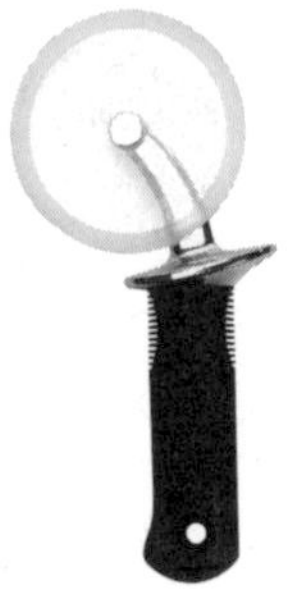
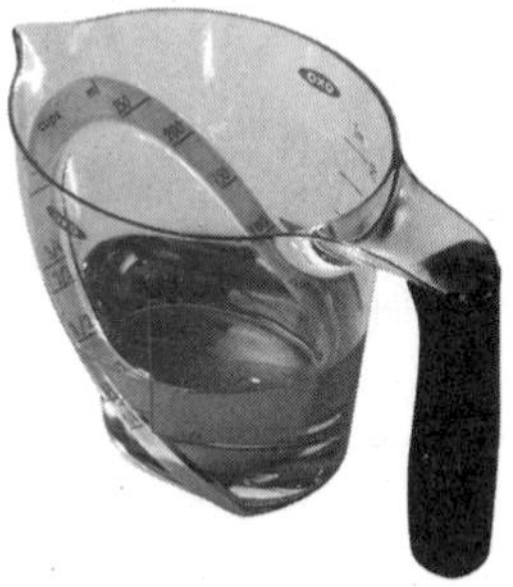
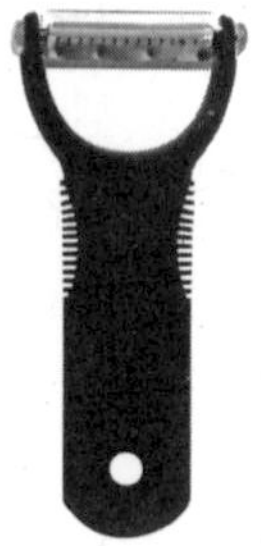
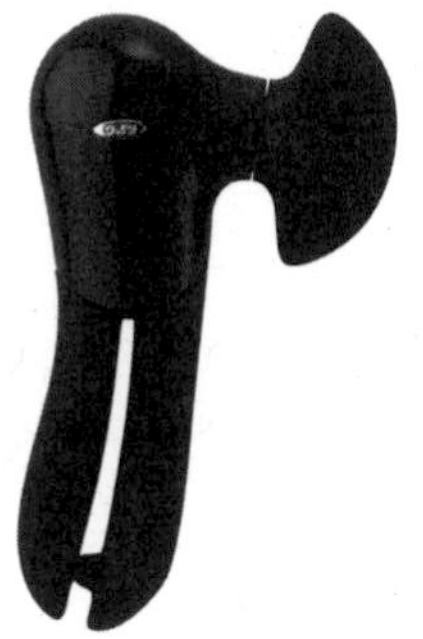
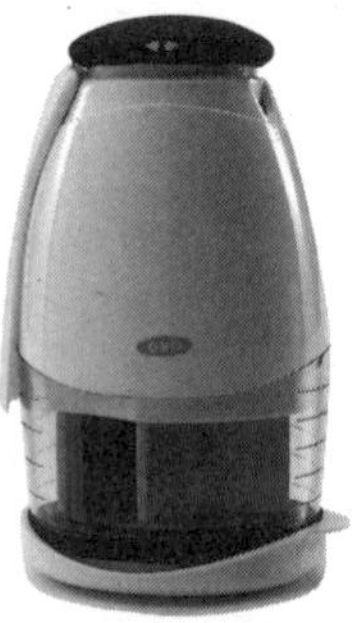
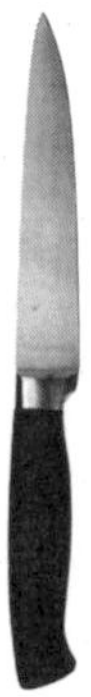
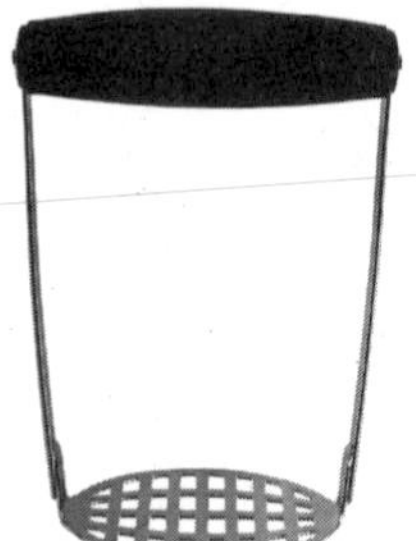
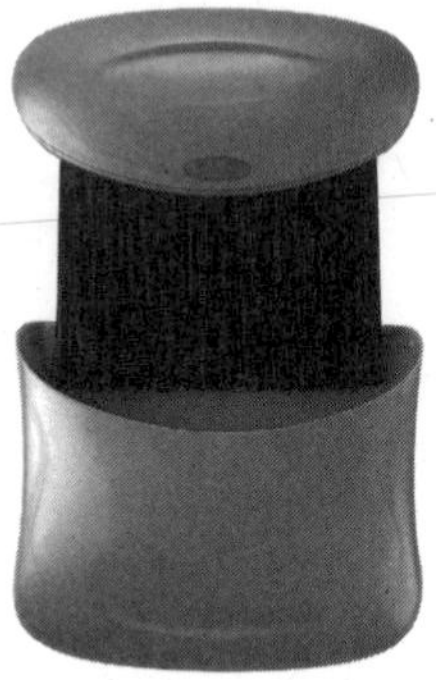
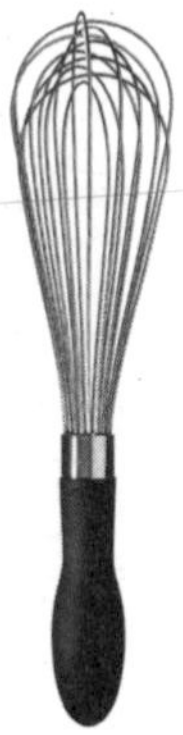

with arthritis. Gadgets came out all the time. Many had employed designs to look cosmetically appealing and were packaged to look great on the display racks in stores. But if you had arthritis, you couldn't use them without pain. All Sam had to do was watch Betsey in the kitchen to realize she was having a bad experience that good design could end.

An idea was now alive. Farber took his idea to a New York design firm he had worked with before; Smart Design. Think hard about Farber's motivation for a bit. He wanted to do something meaningful. And authentic. This was a good idea because there were a lot of people like Betsey who were having increasingly painful experiences when working in the kitchen and trying to use basic culinary tools. It is also poignantly painful for family members to watch someone they love struggle to do the things they used to be able to do with easeful joy. Sam wanted to help as many people as possible, so one of his objectives was to keep the price points low, so the broadest possible group of arthritis sufferers could benefit. To give the designers a vested interest and to keep initial overhead costs low, Farber got Smart Design to put aside its usual fees in exchange for a 3 percent royalty and a small advance.

The design team took their research to the target customers, those who suffered from arthritis. They explored the manual limitations of a variety of people at different ages, looking for factors like declining strength that comes with aging. They considered wrist types, hand motions, and tasks like twisting, pulling, grating, peeling, and squeezing. As they worked, their passion grew until it matched Sam's. The right incentives didn't hurt either. They came up with models and tested them with real subjects until they arrived at an initial three categories of products: squeeze tools, measuring devices, and the gadgets and utensils (such as knives and peelers with the black multipurpose handles you now see so ubiquitously on the store shelves).

The real beauty in all this is that the OXO products are not just good for those with motor limitations, they are easier to use for everybody. They created an approach that was extensible, and could be repeated without loss of innovation. Then they figured out what their design gestalt was about and made sure everything had it. Now, the supply of Good Grips ideas seems endless. And each one carries equity from the others. It is a fantastic example of virtually all the aspects of "FLAVOR."

OXO created an approach that was extensible, and could be repeated without loss of innovation.

The products, as you already know, are a huge success. And, of course, there was the usual bevy of companies that slapped their foreheads and said, "Why didn't we think of that?" Then they rushed to market with variations and darned-near outright copies. But true to the spirit of a design-driven company, OXO was already off to the races with soft-handled Good Grip tea kettles, jar openers, brushes, scrapers, and even easy-to-grip wooden spoons with widened handles. If that made competitors gasp, it wasn't long before OXO had teamed up with the Sierra Club with a line of Good Grip garden tools. And, do you know what? OXO never let up. All you need to do is visit the company's web site (http://www.oxo.com/oxoHome.jsp) to see countless other products that emerge each year to a loyal following that has led to ongoing growth in the face of all competitors.

The integrity of the idea and constantly spinning off fresh products from a pipeline always loaded with new offerings has fended off "knock-off" competitors and kept the original idea fresh and growing even after Farber sold OXO to the General Housewares Corporation in 1992, although he remained as the principal of the firm. Why was it such a success? Because the company was focused, had a long-term approach, was authentic, was vigilant, stayed original, and the design process was repeatable.

As you can see, what we have been talking about as a pathway to success starts with an idea about designing something new and fresh that solves an experiential and perhaps an (as yet) unrecognized need. Then your company gets designed around the fulfillment of your customers' desire for a better experience. You can do it in increments, as a start-up, or by conversion, but when you're finished, you need to be completely committed and keep all the aspects active and working.

If you do, and don't slip, stumble, or lose your way, you will have a company that is resilient to change, that is stimulating to its employees and customers. If you do enough stuff right—take a few risks, make a few mistakes, keep learning and improving—you will find that you have become brilliant at using design to provide an amazing customer experience. Your customers will love you for it!

6

Go Forth
and Matter

We want to thank you for having taken this journey with us for the last couple of hundred pages. We hope that it has been an enlightening experience for you, and that it has helped you understand how great design can take your enterprise to new levels.

We'd like to conclude this offering of ideas and examples by presenting an overarching context. Why does design really matter? Why should you take on the difficult task of re-engineering your company to become design driven? We've shown you examples of how a handful of companies have used design to create enormous success for their business, but what really is the root of the reason of why design could take them there? Well, we believe that there is a higher-level idea that drives all of this.

Over the years, we have found ourselves in conversations organized around the question, "what is it that people really want out of life?." Marketers ask this question and promote their answers. So do psychologists. Theologians of course claim to know. And more than a few of the rest of us seek our own answers every day. It is a complex question, pondered for centuries by individuals and groups more qualified to offer answers than the authors of this book.

This said, however, we do think we know the answer to that question. Or at least an answer that matters to your business. This answer has been given thematically throughout this book. It has been implicit, but now we would now like to explicitly propose it: *People are seeking a great experience of being alive.*

Although some folks seem to go about the seeking in mysterious and even bizarre ways, we nevertheless stand by this idea and the idea that follows: *Human beings do whatever they do based upon an expectation that their experience will be the better for it.* We work and strive to improve our lives for our families and ourselves. We want to make positive use of our time, to accomplish things large and small, to enjoy life and to relax. We want to make every day we can meaningful. And we want to enjoy the ride.

Ask yourself if this seems true. We think you will agree. Humans strive to improve their situation with the ultimate goal of ongoing happiness and joy in their lives. Everything we do, difficult or easy, fun or painful, has something to do with having a better experience of being alive. We want this for us, our loved ones, and on some level for society at large. And along the road traveled, we want to make the actual traveling the best it can be.

Consequently, when it comes to design, you need to start with the design of a superior human experience in your product or service category. What this means is to always consider the human element as primary. And within this to recognize the emotional impact of what you are offering. This seems obvious, but actually it is difficult because of a common paradox: *In business, we*

tend to shy away from most things emotional.
We'd prefer to rationalize, measure, process,
and systematize. Ironically, we tend to put faith
in things that are decidedly not humanistic:
Science. Math. Machines. When the going gets
gray, we sprint for black or white.

But to be great at design, you need to
embrace the human condition and recognize that
when it's all said and done, this is what will serve
you the best. Getting back to that universal
question of *what do we all want from life*, you
need to understand that the experience we have
of the things and places we spend our time with
must be compelling. We want things that are
engaging, fun, personal, useful, productive, and
desirable. And emotionally rewarding.

For a CEO, or Chairman of the Board, all
of this takes a great leap of faith. You will need
to put design in the forefront. *What? You are
asking me to put the blueprint for our company's
future in the hands of a bunch of art school
grads?* We say yes. Because these designers
are the people who will help you understand the
human element in your market and come up with
the ways to delight and satisfy what are often
unarticulated needs. And as we've said, they
cannot do it alone. They need your help even as
you need theirs. Listen to them. They are the
ones who are in touch with human emotion, need,
and desire, and who can translate all this into a
compelling business proposition. They will be the
ones to help you matter.

In closing, we have covered a wide variety
of material in this book, and have offered diverse
examples of success and failure to illustrate our
position. It is all important. If nothing else, we'd

like you to walk away with three important ideas. If you build these ideas into your business and remind yourself of them daily, you are taking the first steps to becoming a design-driven company—one that matters and that people might grow to love.

1. Design matters.

- Great design is the best means of building an indirect relationship with your customers and creating value in their lives. It is how you will connect with them.

- It is about a broader experience that includes nearly everything about you, your products, and services that your customer comes in contact with. We call this the customer experience supply chain.

- It is emotional in nature and must be built with this in mind. Do not shy away from this.

- It should be an authentic yet compelling proposition. Do not try to be someone who you are not. Be who you are, and be a good one.

- Design should be treated as a top strategic element of your business. Few things are more important.

2. Design is a process, not an event.

- Design thinking and process needs to be embedded in everything you do. And happen on a daily basis. You need to live it and believe in it. You need to manage it.

- Design is the responsibility of all. It is not just the job of the designer to put out great design. Great design is everybody's job. Top to bottom, end to end.

- The customer experience supply chain needs to be defined, staffed, led, and managed constantly. It is the lifeblood of your customer's experience—what your customers will see, touch, hear, smell, and feel from you.

- This all requires vision, diligence, and discipline. See point 3 below.

3. If it was easy, everybody would do it.

- It takes significant cultural change to be design driven. You will need to shake up your company top to bottom. Be prepared to find antibodies in your corporate system. Fight them and push onward.

- Doing great design takes time. This is tough in today's world where everything keeps accelerating. But it has to be done right, and this takes time.

- You have to be willing to do the hard work. The best customer solution is often the most difficult to develop and implement. But this has to be your focus. It will get easier after the first few times.

- You will make mistakes. No doubt. This happens to everybody, *including Apple!* Just learn from them and get better.

- It takes money. No way around it.

- You have to have faith and commitment. The first time it blows up, don't give up. Stick with it. It will work eventually.

- Trust your gut and understanding of the human condition. After all, you're human too—aren't you?

We wish you and your customers the very best of times. It really is all about the experience, and great experience, while often serendipitous, is predictably provided by great design. Do this well, and people will be most inclined to love you and your company. You will matter.

Endnotes

Chapter 3

1 Leander Kahney, "Inside Look at Birth of the iPod," *Wired*, 21 July 2004.

2 Tom Hornby and Dan Knight, "A History of the iPod," *Orchard*, September 2007.

3 Janice Steinberg, "The 800-lb. Gorilla," *San Diego Union–Tribune*, 19 January 2006.

4 Marty Neumeier, *The Brand Gap: How to Bridge the Distance Between Business Strategy and Design* (Peachpit Press, 2005).

Chapter 4

5 Lewis P. Carbone, *Clued In: How to Keep Customers Coming Back Again and Again* (Pearson, 2004).

6 www.designmuseum.org/design/jonathan-ive.

7 Frank Rose, "Seoul Machine," *Wired*, May 2005.

8 Ibid.

9 www.gallup.com/poll/.

10 Target Corporation, http://sites.target.com/images/corporate/about/pdfs/cor_factcard_101107.pdf), 10 October 2007.

11 See Wikipedia for the back-story.

12 Jennifer Wells, "Can Starbucks Go with the Flow?" www.theglobeandmail.com, 8 February 2008.

13 "Coffee break for Starbucks' 135,000 baristas: Coffee chain to close all 7,100 stores for employee training. Dunkin' Donuts offers 99 cent promotion," CNNMoney.com, 26 February 2008.

14 Wally Bock, "Alas, Poor Polaroid, I Knew Them …," *Monday Memo*, 22 October 2001.

15 www.stanford.edu/group/dschool/.

16 "Tomorrow's B-School? It Might Be a D-School," *BusinessWeek*, 1 August 2005.

Chapter 5

17 Gary McWilliams, "Can Circuit City Survive Boss's Cure?" *Wall Street Journal*, 11 February 2006.

Chapter 6

18 http://www1.shopping.com/xPR-Haier-XQG65-11SU.

19 Dan Tynan, "The 25 Worst Tech Products of All Time," *PCWorld*, www.pcworld.com/article/id,125772-page,1/article.html, 26 May 2006.

20 Robert Archer, "THX to Launch Video Training Program," www.cepro.com/article/thx_to_launch_video_training_program/K320, 24 January 2008.

21 http://buzzfeed.com/buzz/Fuego_BBQ_Grill.

22 Sara Hart, "Fuego Grill," *Dwell Daily*, www.dwell.com/daily/techblog/8664762.html, 23 July 2007.

23 Michael Bergdahl and Rob Walton, *The 10 Rules of Sam Walton: Success Secrets for Remarkable Results* (Wiley, 2006).

24 http://seekingalpha.com, posted 23 May 2006.

25 Ibid.

26 Ohlin Associates, www.ohlinassociates.com/press_room_experience_matters.aspx, 21 May 2007.

27 Ibid.

28 Kit Hinrichs and Delphine Hirasuna of @Issue: Journal of Business and Design contributed to original research on this story.

Chapter 7

29 Mike Elgan, "New Rugged Dell—the Anti-Air," *Computerworld* blogs, http://blogs.computerworld.com/new_rugged_dell_the_anti_air, 4 March 2008.

30 Angus MacKenzie, "This Much I Know: Adrian Van Hooydonk, Head of Design BMW Brand," *Motor Trend*, www.motortrend.com/features/consumer/112_0606_adrian_van_hooydonk_bmw.html.

31 Ibid.

Chapter 8

32 *Fast Company Staff*, www.fastcompany.com/magazine/119/the-seven-axioms-of-yves.html, 28 September 2007.

Index

D

E

I

J